The Day The South African Constitutional Court Legalised Crime and Corruption— To the benefit of the Guptas.

by Sejake Petrus Motaung

RoseDog Books

PITTSBURGH, PENNSYLVANIA 15238

RoseDog Books
585 Alpha Drive
Suite 103
Pittsburgh, PA 15238
Visit our website at www.rosedogbookstore.com

ISBN: 978-1-6470-2122-1
eISBN: 978-1-6470-2141-2

Table of Contents:

Influenced Prosecutorial Decisions
The Righteousness of Jesus Christ

The Role of the Church
The Jesus Prayer

Birth Right

The Impact of legal crime and the reasons for the
The Reasons behind forming the ConCourt
Standard evidence in the Zondo Commission
Then lightning Struck

The role of ANCWL

Zuma considering another appeal

Subsequently, a number of questions come to mind

The Church of Christ

Ill-discipline at our schools

Cash-in-transit heists and scud missiles

The Three River Dry Clean Murders

Hard-core-facts in the Ace Magashule garage issue

The second garage transaction in Bloemfontein

Equality before the eyes of Society

South Africa Belong to All who live in it

Police action or inaction

Incidents in the past

Dogs mating

A Benoni man relieving himself

A child in a crèche

A baby shot at the back of the mother

A Court sanctioned deviation from the law

Service delivery protests

The mind of a rapist

Black on Black violence

Blacks and Whites in Marikana

Conclusion

Mandela and the Jesus mirror

Recommendations

We need to forgive those who wronged us

Go to the Lord and you will live

Abolish the 0ffice of the Public Protector

Abolish the Constitutional Court

Standard Bank and Afri-forum

The standard of the law degree in South Africa

Ramaphosa to be President up to 2024 and beyond

A Sea of Shells

The Stump

Ingonyama Trust

Acknowledgements:

I WANT TO THANK THE FOLLOWING PEOPLE.

My children, Thabang and Molelekeng. You are the apple of my eye and will always treasure being your father.

My Pastor, Reverend Peter Loving. Man of God, you have been a mentor to me and nurtured my spiritual life and my calling. The Reverend OJ Thebe for advising me to study through Theological Education by Extension College. It is at this College that some of the intriguing questions I had about Jesus Christ were answered.

The entire Boipatong congregation of Uniting Reformed Church in Southern Africa, URCSA. In particular, the Boitumelo branch in Sebokeng where I am stationed by the Church Council. We are like one big family and we share the spiritual food in the presence of Jesus Christ. You have developed in me a sense of belonging.

My friend Moses Punki Nteso. We have gone through many huddles together and may the Good Lord sustain your endurance as He did in me.

TEE College in Turffontein. Before I enrolled with you, I knew very little about Jesus Christ. I must admit that although I knew about

God, it has been difficult to incorporate Jesus Christ in my Christian belief. It was in pursuance of knowing who Jesus is, that I ended up studying until I graduated. The initial plan was to equip myself for preaching only. It soon became clear that the more I thought I know the less I realised I knew nothing. I certainly could not teach if I knew half of what I was supposed to deliver.

Last but not least, Jesus Christ, for saving my life from ruin and restoring me.

Introduction:

"We expect you to stand on guard not only against direct assault on the principles of the constitution, but against insidious corrosion. Attacks on the basic rights of the people are invariably couched in innocent language."

-Nelson Mandela speech at the inauguration of the
Constitutional Court, 14 February 1995.

The narrative in this book is drawn from three primary sources.

Firstly, the speech by Nelson Rolihlahla Mandela at the inauguration of the South African Constitutional Court, quoted in part in the introduction above. That document has been attached at the back of the book. I have numbered the sentences in this speech, for ease of reference. Secondly, from various Newspaper clips. It must be stressed that it is assumed that at the time of printing and the facts there-in have not been proved wrong, then they are correct. If the evidence is later taken up in court and proved incorrect, I apologise unreservedly. Lastly, from the Bible.

This book seeks to answer a number of questions, the first being how does South Africa find itself on the brink of recession? With the concomitant poverty, unemployment, rampant crime and corruption, while we have a Constitutional Court.

1. The reasons for its formation, which relate to its functions.
2. The model institution that Nelson Mandela had in mind when he came up with the idea of the inception of a Constitutional Court.
3. Does it fulfil its mandate as discussed and agreed with Nelson Mandela?
4. Most importantly, do we as South Africans, still need this Institution? Considering Mandela's speech, second line in the quote above about 'innocent language.'
5. Evidence emanating from the numerous commissions of inquiry in relation to Mandela quote above.

"…obey my voice and I will be your God, and you shall be my people, and walk in all the way that I command you and it may be well with you, (Jeremiah 7: 23-38)

Jesus Christ said, "For I say to you, unless your righteousness exceeds the righteousness of the Scribes and Pharisees, you shall by no means enter the Kingdom of Heaven", (Matthew 5: 20 JCM Bible).

With such prophetic words from God, we stand with amazement at the crime and lawless situation that South Africa finds itself in. We can only ask in amazement, South Africans, where did we go wrong? Especially after the hard work incurred in realising democracy. However there is no hope lost, provided we return to God and as His word says above, we walk in the way He commands us.

1

Many Religions

We have many religions in the world that all use God and gods to a variable degree. The one God I am referring to is the Father of the risen Jesus Christ, (1 John 4: 15). The one and only Jesus Christ who through the Holy Spirit rose from the grave.

The Mind of the Writer:

This book is written by a deeply Christian South African inspired by the Holy Spirit. It is not about Jacob Zuma, but definitely about how corruption and crime festered during his administration. The Auditor General Kimi Makwethu corroborates this fact under the heading "Why it's getting worse, the Auditor-General blames state capture during the Jacob Zuma years for increased looting at the municipal level, and welcomes steps to counter it," City Press, page 6, on 27 May 2018.

It is written in the first person. Firstly because it's to a large extend, a true story. It is about what happened and is still happening. One cannot write in the third person as if it's fiction. Secondly because it affects politicians. When you speak to a politician you don't say, 'your male parent', it's discriminatory, you say, your father.

A combination of factors like the interpretation of court verdicts, actions taken by law enforcement officers and the behaviour of the South African public have influenced the state of affairs we find ourselves in.

I must say on the outright that no attempt has been made to engage scientific legal methods of investigation to dispute actions so taken. The approach that I used in the assessment of the declining moral compass in South Africa is as follows: this is the misconduct that occurred, the police and the entire criminal justice system, the South African community were active or inactive towards it in the following manner, subsequently the courts responded to it in this manner, referring to the verdicts, or based on the inaction of the police, the courts could do nothing hence the community was left to perceive the misconduct in the best manner they could interpret. Therefore, based on the action or inaction, the ordinary citizen should behave in the following manner going forward.

Alternatively, one can say this storyline has nothing to do with what Act Number X, read in conjunction with subsection Y (iii) of Act Z, states; therefore this is what the verdict should have been. Be that as it may, I have drawn as much as applicable from the Bible while quoting newspapers regarding crime and corruption that was committed.

This, taking into cognizance that whether there was a verdict or no verdict, a message is send to the people, from the most educated to the most illiterate, the one who has never seen the back of a classroom door at all.

I am a strong believer in the efficacy and integrity of law enforcement officers, from Judges, right down to foot soldiers patrolling our streets. How they behave is what determines my moral stance in particular, acts of crime. Not only mine but, I believe, the entire community of South Africa. Nevertheless, there is a perceived despondency towards our criminal justice system, stemming particularly from the past nine years, 9 May 2009-14 February 2018, where Jacob Zuma, was President of South Africa.

To illustrate the point I am making, I wish to cite a few examples. In the Sowetan Newspaper, 20 April 2018 page 6, a story was published with a heading, "Duduzane, (former President Jacob Zuma's son) to face court over crash". Allegations are that Duduzane Zuma crashed his vehicle, a Porche, into a stationary taxi wherein Phumzile Dube was travelling. This incident, which occurred four year ago resulted in her death.

The paper continues "Despite recommendations made by magistrate Lalitha Chetty that Duduzane Zuma should be prosecuted, the NPA (National Prosecuting Authority) refused to charge him. The first, among the many, interesting questions here is the semantics of the word, refuse. Why would an arm of the law refuse to obey a court order? Does the law exempt them from obeying this instruction? It poses an interesting quagmire as everybody in South Africa is charged if an accident results in the death of a person.

Pedzisane Dube, Phumzile's brother raises a concern which is basically a motivation for putting pen on paper to compile this book. He says, "This means that the South African justice system works…" (That means, up until that incident it was perceived not working). A system for it to be called a system has an inherent and an unavoidable trait of 'continuously working'. If there is doubt that it is not working it means there is a breakdown somewhere which needs to be investigated and corrected.

As a result, the inaction of the NPA in this case has elicited the following remark from Phumlane's sickly mother, "I have lost an interest in this story…and I do not want to know anything about the case because it exacerbates my illness". This frustration can be gleaned from the general South African public. If there can be a similar incident befalling another family, it will not be far-fetched to think that they will comment, 'what's the point in reporting, seeing that the Dubes' were shunned.

The Sunday Times, 22 April 2018 page 20, also sheds some insight in the thinking towards the NPA performing its job. In the comment about the NPA taking three years to prosecute Julius Malema, the leader of Economic Freedom Fighters party, for corruption and money laundering allegations and the subsequent action or perceived inaction against him, it states, "This has again highlighted the importance of a prosecuting authority that acts without fear or favour". The Sunday Times, also putting the story of Phumlane into the spotlight, continues, "The NPA, until this week, flatly refused to prosecute Duduzane, (mark the injunction, flatly refused to prosecute him), even when a judicial inquest found that there was prima facie evidence that his negligent driving led to Dube's death". Duduzane Zuma was acquitted of this offence on 12 July 2019.

Influenced Prosecutorial Decisions

The Sunday Times assigns an appropriate heading towards this dubious behaviour of this organ of law enforcement, and it says, "NPA still bending under political breeze". The commentary proceeds with the rather distressing state of affairs that South Africans are still looking forward to the dawn of a period where the NPA will do its job free from political interference. "The NPA, since its inception, has been riddled by scandals and allegations that its senior prosecutors are aligned to different camps in the African National Congress, (ANC), and that this often influences prosecutorial decisions". These influenced decisions, by implication have a profound bearing on the court verdicts.

The phrase, 'Influenced prosecutorial decisions' referred to by Sunday Times is what I have observed myself and has prompted me to develop a keen interest in such decisions.

The long held suspicions were confirmed in news that appeared in the City Press, 28 April 2018 page 1, under the heading, "How Busi saved Ace." This refers to the Public Protector who, because of a misunderstanding on the report by her predecessor Thuli Madonsela exonerated the then Free State Premier Ace Magashule from any wrong doing. The report was about the R220, some reports say 250, million rand allocated to the Estina Dairy farm meant to improve the economic conditions of poor blacks in Vrede. This despite the fact that she could have sought clarity from the writer of the report, Advocate Thuli Madonsela. South Africa is witnessing a peculiar state of affairs where R250million has vanished out of the coffers of those who held this account and nobody knows what happened. (As I have stated above, Busisiwe Mkhwebane flatly denies Ace Magashule is implicated in the report before her.)

Dubious prosecutorial decisions originate from the time Jacob Zuma was accused of corruption when, it is alleged, he received a bribe from a French arms company in the 1997. The allegation is that, Schabir Shaik facilitated the transfer.

Be that as it may, it is still a puzzle from Mars how Jacob Zuma and Shabir Shaick were accused of the same crime but only Shaick was put to trial and convicted. To add salt to the wound, the evidence, in the form of spy tapes, on the basis of which, Zuma had to be put to trial, were whisked away to some Island and only retrieved when the Democratic Alliance, (DA) made a court application for their retrieval.

This poses yet another intricate legal mess, especially for a law abiding citizen. Questions arise, regarding to who took those tapes away? Under what legal permission or right? Is it not an offence to conceal evidence? Shouldn't the culprit be charged? With the e-technology so advanced nowadays, had those tapes not been tampered with and sifted off the incriminating evidence? Does an ordinary South African citizen also have the right to conceal evidence, with the concomitant impunity? Last but not least, what moral influence does this present to the community?

This because we are already sitting with a number of cases that were handled in a suspicious manner. Talk about a roller coaster of ineptitudes. For instance:

The Life Esidimeni Home for the mentally handicapped patients in Gauteng, where patients were moved to ill-equipped NGO's and later died, over a period of months. In compensation to the families, the government had to fork out millions of rand but no one has been prosecuted, so far.

The Bank of Lisbon, which mysteriously caught fire, starting from the top floor where it is alleged the offices of the Gauteng Provincial Government Health Department are situated. This is the Department that the public thought was supposed to give a litany of events leading to the Life Esidimeni saga. Despite repeated reassurances from the Health MEC, on television, that nothing untoward can be suspected, the public is still waiting for investigative report on what caused the fire. So the suspicion that the fire was a deliberate plot from those implicated in corruption in Life Esidimeni, still stands.

Similarly, in the Emfuleni Local Municipality in the Vaal, the offices in Duncanville that housed the electricity department also mysteriously caught fire when Jacob Khawe, an ANC member, now the Provincial Secretary,was deployed to investigate corruption in this Municipality, started probing it. A report is still coming, hopefully...

In Cape Town we have numerous incidents of trains that were burnt and so far no one has been arrested at the time of writing. While in Cape Town, this is the town described as a world leader in murder crime. Our constitution guarantees a right to life, but Cape Town seems to be an exception to this rule. This city, is also the world leader, not only in murder rate but in unsolved murder cases. Add to this high incidents of raped and murdered women as well as numerous cash in-transit heists.

As a result, because of these incidents that give evidence of people losing their lives and no plans being in place to stop them, I could not resist the urge to involve God's Word, in the interpretation of our verdicts or put relevantly, the entire criminal justice system. I have involved and analysed the criminal state of South Africa under the background of what it would have been like, had the law enforcement officers and the entire population, engaged Jesus Christs' teachings in dealing with crime in general.

In the book of Luke 4: 18-19, Jesus states clearly how He is empowered by the Holy Spirit to dispense the Good News. The Good News He refers to involve the setting free of those in captivity, the recovery of the sight of the blind, including Spiritual blindness and to free the oppressed. This He will do in the Kingdom of God that is here on earth, and on the fullness of time, referring to the Judgement Day.

The Righteousness of Jesus Christ

In the book of Matthew 5: 6, Jesus stresses the word righteousness, (The Maxwell Leadership Bible) "Blessed are those who hunger and thirst for righteousness". This righteousness, he further qualifies, as I have stated above, in verse 20 of the same chapter.

The desire for righteousness on earth and in particular South Africa, is what, again, inspired the writing of this piece of work. Righteousness which derives its origin from the Greek word, dikaiosune, does not only involve doing the right things or taking the right decisions. But involves, in tandem fairness, equality and justice. Strong's Concordance goes on to describe dikaiosune as justness and divine righteousness.

In other words justice as a derivative of dikaiosune, cannot be what it is supposed to be, unless it involves God in its embodiment. There's a divine reason for this. When God, 'The I Am', (Exodus 3: 14) send Moses to Pharaoh, it was because of the cry of injustice meted out by the Egyptians to the Israelites which had reverberated into the entire Heaven and shook God from His Throne. Take note of this, "I have surely seen the oppression of my people…and have heard their cry…" (Exodus 3: 7 JC Maxwell). Again there is a divine reason for this reaction from God, all human beings are made in the likeness and image of God, (Genesis 1: 26 JC Maxwell) and there is absolutely no justification for one to exploit another.

Jesus Christ gives an illustration of justness in the parable of the un-forgiving debtor, (Matthews 18: 21-35). After the said king settled amicably, the debts of two men who could not pay their arrears, justice, had to be dispensed, through a retrial by the same king, of the man who could not "do to the other man, who owed him, as it was done unto him", (Matthews 7: 12).

If our politicians could for once, imagine themselves in the shoes of those they exploit, or put correctly, did to us as they would have it done unto them, South Africa would resume its rightful stature of being the envy of the world it once was during the time of Nelson Mandela. Nelson Mandela is gone, Jesus is here and will be here eternally.

Jesus goes on, in the same verse that this principle is enacted by the prophets and so applies to all in the world. In other words, this prophecy tells us of dire consequences should we deviate from it.

For one thing, it is not well in SA for any law abiding citizen. On the contrary it is like the 'Promised Land' to criminals.

As the law stands now, expressing an opinion on a court verdict is tantamount to committing suicide. However as a Christian, I feel duty bound to voice an opinion on behalf of Jesus Christ who stands shoulder high as the Lord and Saviour of all those who yearn for an everlasting Kingdom of God. "Bear one another's burdens, and so fulfil the Law of Christ", (Galatians 6: 2). That is what I long for, the law of Christ, and I believe is the aspiration of every law abiding citizen.

When I started writing this book, I was praying like Elijah when he said, "Oh Lord...prove now that you are God of Israel...and I have done all this, at your command... answer me Lord, answer me, so that these people will know you are God and you want them back to yourself", (1 Kings 18: 36-37). After Elijah said this prayer, God sent fire to the world that changed the course of people who worshipped idols, at the behest of Ahab and Jezebel and started worshiping God, the Father of Jesus Christ, (John 14: 20-21 JCM).

Crime and lawlessness gnaw our country to shreds. I can only conclude that, we South Africans, do not love our country. The country we normally sang and sing about in our National Anthem, "Nkosi sikele I'Africa....we shall live and die for you South Africa". This cry has now become a lip service. It no longer comes from the bottom of our hearts, as we cried during the days of Apartheid.

For example, we are just too happy to connive, with anybody from anywhere in the world, to destroy this country through a menace like 'nyaope' fed to our children. We need to pray, as I do every day, that Jesus Christ help us that whoever manufactures these drugs should her/himself eat them so that they do not reach our children. They should eat the entire stock so that our children are safe from this peril.

Institutions that had a dramatic impact on moral turbulence in SA are: The Church of Christ, The ANCWL, the general public and the Criminal Justice System. However, it was difficult to discuss them separately as sometimes they act on their own and at times simultaneously.

The Role of the Church:

Fake Prophets. One of the disasters facing South Africa is the emergence of fake prophets. Briefly, it is not difficult for members of the public, to determine if a prophecy is indeed a message from God, as all sermons should be.

The Bible is the Word of God. But the tricky part is always the interpretation of this Word of God. Three of the basic methods, and by no means not the only ones, that people can use to test if indeed the message is from God are:

God takes the LEAD in whatever action He wants people to embark on:

One example out of the many is that, Jesus told everyone that whoever wants to follow Him, should carry His Cross, (Luke 9: 23, JCM). The reason being that He carried it first Himself. So if members of the public are called upon to drink, eat, and smear whatever is said to effect a cure, that Prophet must start the act before anybody else. I've seen people eating scary objects while the said prophet does not. If people have cockroaches on their faces, the prophet must for the entire duration of the service apply the insecticide on his/her face first, and only on the following church session or Sunday, can she/he apply it to the congregation. As this is done for financial prosperity, that wealth must be visible to her/him without the congregation having to tithe.

Secondly, God in Jesus Christ and the Holy Spirit, will never contradict Himself. A prophecy that so and so is bewitching people, (O a loya, in Sesotho, U ya thakatha, in isi-Zulu) is a hate sermon and does not come from God but from the devil who is out to sow confusion and hatred. This because God who expects you to "love your enemies…" (Matthew 5: 44-45), cannot lead you to hate that enemy by telling you she/he is the cause of your misfortunes. What God promises all of us throughout the Bible is that He will protect, bless us and fight all our battles, "Come to Me you who labour and are heavy laden…" (Matthew 11: 28 JCM). You will never and I say it again never truly love a person you are told caused your hardship through witchcraft. At best you can only pretend.

As an illustration to this Divine principle: Recently a well-known prophet, Sheperd Bushiri, is said to have prophesied that some other man's wife is bewitched by her mother-in-law: The Star 14 March 2018, p2. This allegation led to the man's family ending in a divorce court and the marriage being annulled. In the Book of Malachi 2: 16ff, God says "I hate divorce…" fortunately it comes before the text on tithing, 3: 10. Now the word hate means, I do not want it, no matter how valid your reasons. Alternatively, I understand your reasons, all the same I hate it. The only way to justify the authenticity of this prophecy is if we agree that God made a mistake. Now a god that makes mistakes and, worst still, forgets what he said is definitely not Jehovah. God cannot hate divorce and lead you to that same divorce. What the sovereign God will do, through Jesus Christ is, He will redirect that curse back to your enemy.

Therefore do justice to your marriage, do not divorce.

The logical assessment is that the prophecy was definitely not from God.

"God keeps every promise He has made…If you claim that God said something which He never said, He will reprimand you and show that you are a liar," (Proverbs 30: 5-6 GNB). According to Jesus righteousness, the Word of God must be distributed fairly and do justice to those who assimilate it so that people are transformed not reformed.

The Jesus Prayer:

This is the prayer that Jesus ordained as the Prayer God answers and it is found in Luke 18: 9-14, "God be merciful to me a sinner". In this text, we need to observe, the level of humbleness. First the sinner stood far off, not raising his eyes to Heaven but garnered enough courage to approach Jesus. This is the prayer Jesus said is approved by God and is answered because of the utmost humility shown by the one saying it.

Anybody can say it, not only the prophets, anybody, and it will be answered. It is in stark contrast to the prayer said by the Pharisee next to this humble man. It is also what we observe in the churches nowadays, where Jesus is hauled like he has no final decision and is bound to answer favourably. A prayer like 'Hey Jesus come and bless me, I have paid my R1million tithe, which You said I need to pay, I have fasted as you commanded and I'm wondering when are you going to bless me,' is just not on. Sometimes we observe how hurriedly a prayer is said so that people do not leave before they visit the Automatic Teller Machine, sometimes situated in the Church building. This is the reason people tithe but are getting poorer. Tithing is of crucial importance in the Church of Christ, make no mistake. However, the attitude plays equally a crucial role as Jesus Himself says in His ensuing comments after the prayers of the two men. The reason for tithing is just as important, if it is for buying luxury cars and aeroplanes it is just as futile because "all that will vanish into thin air", read Ecclesiastes 1:2; 10: 14; and12: 8. These words were written by the most intelligent and richest man ever to grace these shores, King Solomon, son of King David.

A word of advice to all and sundry is, let's study our Bibles and ask the Holy Spirit to help us in interpreting the Word of God. Anti-Christ has arrived, "For some godless people have slipped in among us unnoticed… and deny our only God and our Lord Jesus Christ" (Jude 1: 4). This is the scenario, of anti-Christ, in South Africa today.

Last but not least, keep in mind that you can fool everybody, but you can't fool Jesus Christ, because "God searches the heart…" (Jeremiah 17: 10)

Forgiveness:

"Moreover if your brother sins against you…And if he refuses to hear them, tell it to the church. But if he refuses… let him be to you like a heathen and a tax collector,"

(Matthew 18: 15-17).

"Repay no evil for evil,"

(Romans 12: 17)

When South Africa abandoned Apartheid, it realised that reconciliation will be impossible without Forgiveness. This was done through the setting up of the TRC, (Truth and Reconciliation Commission) that was chaired by Bishop Desmond Tutu and the late Dr Alex Boraine. When they reached the conclusion of the mandate of that structure, to hand all the reigns to the ruling party it was because, with the evidence that was presented, blacks and whites could shake hands and forget about the past. You cannot forgive if you do not forget, although the usual rhetoric is, forgive but do not forget.

I wish to add that forgiveness does not compel anybody to sit around the table and enjoy a cup of tea with whoever was regarded as an enemy. While it would be a good gesture, it cannot be a pre or after-care condition. If there are those, blacks or whites who feel aggrieved by the peace that was brokered, it would do them good to accept majority decision. We have gone past the era of judging a person by the colour of her/his skin.

However it is a fundamental truism that we have people who still perceive others as kaffirs or a boers, foreigners and nationals and the latest phenomenon where people regard others as sub-human or animals to be destroyed. This shows how difficult it is to come to grips with the concept of forgiveness, particularly if one was the victim of the atrocity. It puts us in better position to comprehend and embrace the grace of God in affording us His Son to die for us. Because without Him, forgiveness is impossible.

To give a demonstration of how impossible forgiveness is without repentance, which is a challenge to some of our political leaders, one has to assess how Jesus Christ treated two of His disciples, Judas Iscariot and Saul, who was later known as St Paul. One can even conclude that in Judas Iscariot, Jesus wanted to bring to light that a person can be as hard as a stone and resist change. This man Judas, after being with Jesus his entire life and observed the power of healing and forgiveness from Him, appreciated miracles like walking on the water, quelling the rough seas, enjoyed a free meal initially meant for a few people but was miraculously augmented to feed thousands, free boat cruising, realised the repentance of those Jesus met and many more miracles, still saw a bumper lotto of R30.00 in Jesus' death instead of surrendering to Him. Meaning, to Judas Iscariot, the entire act of Grace to millions of people was worth R30.00.

He could have asked Jesus to tell the fish to cough out the R30.00, (Mathews 17: 24-27). Ironically, when Judas left Jesus on the table, (John 13: 30), He had just washed his, (Judas) feet, (John 13: 1ff) before

He confronted him with the revelation of deceitfulness in his heart. (John 13: 18ff). But the man flatly refused to repent. What more could Jesus do?

In contrast, a sinful Saul experienced one transforming miracle from Jesus, (Acts 9: 1-19) on him and that was enough. The rest is history. Paul is the writer of 13 of the 27 Books of the New Testament. Some say 14 if we add the book of Hebrews. My point is, Jesus could have done to Judas Iscariot what He did to Saul. The question is why HE did not? It is because Jesus was making us aware that in this world, there are people who will not repent or ask for forgiveness, no matter what you do to appease them, and (The reader must please note that this is only my interpretation). South Africa is faced with such people today, and to be able to realise a prosperous and economically viable country we need to move past these people. Blacks and white South Africans have had their differences in the past and by coming together and working side by side much can be achieved.

Birth right

Secondly, Jesus reaction to Judas goes a long way to show that He is the Son of God and IN God, because He did to Judas and Paul exactly what God did to Esau and Jacob. God sanctioned Jacob's blessings by his father Isaac even though Isaac meant it for Esau (Genesis 27: 1-10), because Esau's heart was unrepentant, even while he was in his mother's womb, (Genesis 25: 22). One way of interpreting Genesis 27: 1-10, is that Isaac's effort was destined to fail because God had already blessed Jacob; in Genesis 25: 23. Consider the Words that God uses "One people shall be stronger than the other; and the older shall serve the younger," are the same words that Isaac uses, in rightfully blessing Jacob, even though according to him, Isaac, he was blessing Esau, in Genesis 27: 28-29. If we take into consideration that God is sovereign and answerable to no one, Jacob was already blessed when he was in front of his father. The question may be asked, where does Isaac get the prophetic words he uses on Jacob? The Bible does not say, but we can conclude, with utmost caution that, at the time when Isaac approached the Lord, (Genesis 25: 21). Details of this meeting may be summarised as follows, and The Lord said to Isaac, 'your wife is conceiving twins now as I'm talking to you, "and the Lord granted his plea," bless one of them.' That is why Isaac knew he had to bless one child but did not know which one. On the other hand Rebecca was forced to seek help from the Lord. That meeting resulted in her knowing that the blessed child is Jacob, Verse 23 above. One may say, because Isaac and Rebecca never prayed together, they ended up one having the right hand shoe while the other had the left shoe and none of them knew the shoe's partner is on the other side of the bed. Not only this, but it does sound a reasonable interpretation that none of them, Isaac and Rebecca, ever discussed this, not only miraculous but mind-gnawing encounter with the Lord, until the children were at a ripe age, of anything beyond 20 years. If one assumes a person can only hunt alone, Esau, if he is beyond this age, Genesis 27: 3.

If they prayed together, one assumes Isaac could have mentioned in his prayer that the Lord reveal who of the children should be blessed, to which Rebecca would have provided the answer. Conversely, Rebecca could have inquired of the Lord that the children being twins, why does God bless only one instead of both, to this Isaac could have thanked his wife for unravelling his riddle. However the way Lord revealed this encounter within this family reveals the consistency of the Lord, Genesis 2: 24, "and they shall be one flesh." When the Lord has a mission for a family, to him it does not matter whether His message is delivered to husband or wife, to Him both are equal. Both must help each other to accomplish His mission. Now imagine if you are divorced and part of the answer to your nagging problem is with divorced spouse. 'A family that prays together, stays together,' Anonymous. This can be extended to a young ad executive Al Scalpone, who in 1947 said, "A world at prayer is a world at peace."

We can further learn something from this family and repent. Esau and Jacob lived a life of cat and dog with Esau hell bend on killing his brother Jacob. Why am I saying this is because the Bible says, "As soon as Isaac had finished blessing Jacob and Jacob had scarcely gone out from the presence of Isaac his father, that Esau his brother came in from hunting," Genesis 27: 30. It is a good guess that had Esau found Jacob in the room with his blind father giving away what he, Esau, perceived to be his blessing, he could have killed Jacob there and then. Just like Caine killed his brother Abel, Genesis 4. All this could have been avoided had it not been because of a patriarchal father and matriarchal mother. However, by grace, he couldn't because when God blesses, the blessing is forever, Romans 11: 29.

We can again conclude, again my interpretation and you are entitled to yours, God had twofold mission about Esau and Jacob. First, Jacob's blessing was because the Lord wanted to use his name for Himself, Exodus 3: "The God of Abraham, Isaac and Jacob." Secondly, because there was something devious about Esau and God wanted Esau to experience a remarkable transformation. Verse 30 of Genesis 27, reveal that he took almost the same time to hunt a wild animal, as Jacob who took his from his father's kraal. Unless Esau got this wild animal from a refrigerator, which is doubtful that refrigerators were available in those primitive times, we are inclined to believe he got it by underhanded means, meaning he stole it from some farmer around there. It takes anything from a full day to catch a wild animal.

There are parents in South Africa today, who enjoy their children's loot without even a nerve of asking were they got them. This despite the parent being fully aware that the child is not working. The child's bad behaviour is only exposed when the entire township is taking the law into its hand, when he is accused of stealing or house breakings, sometimes going to the extent of killing the perpetrator. All Isaac and Rebecca had to do was to bless Jacob and take Esau to God for his share of blessing. Isaac was saved from being made a sacrifice by his father's faith in the consistent God, Genesis 22: 12-13. The Bible is the Word of God in which God uses characters in there to teach us about His power and grace. Someone may say stupid Isaac and Rebecca, but we are more stupid because we do not become wiser from the stupidity of others.

To resume our discussion on Esau and Judas Iscariot. Thirdly and most critically, Esau despised his birth right, (Genesis 25: 34 JCM), The Good News Bible explains it better, "That was all Esau cared about his right as the first-born son". That is how Judas devalued himself, from an Apostle to a criminal.

A question may arise how did Esau do it? Genesis 25: 31-32, we read Jacob asked Esau to cede his right as an elder brother; and you know what, Esau agreed. One may well ask, if Esau could sell his entire self for a plate of porridge, how was he going to treat the enormous blessings and wealth that God had for him? There's a TV programme titled 'How I blew it.' It could have started with Esau.

Is this not what we as South Africans did when we ceded our birth right to the Guptas with the assistance of Jacob Zuma and the heartless ANCWL? So determined was ANCWL to have Jacob Zuma as President, so that he can facilitate this hand-over that they threatened to go naked in the streets of Johannesburg if Jacob Zuma was not acquitted for the rape charge. The very women who were fighting tooth and nail to have Jacob Zuma acquitted, are the very once who were in the forefront of corruption and looting in the Jacob Zuma administration.

The full extent of what South Africa did by giving the Guptas our birth right can only be correctly comprehended if one remembers the difficult life Nelson Mandela endured only for Jacob Zuma to rubbish all that.

A lesson to us, love and respect what God gave us. How do you do that? Love God and your fellow sister/brother with the love you love yourself, (Matthew 22: 34-40). Esau did not love himself, (Hebrew 12: 16-17; Malachi 1: 2-3).

"We have sinned and sinned only against you God" (Psalm 51: 4). When Nathan rebuked David's sin, (Greek word for sin is hamartia-missing the mark), he said why have you despised the commandment of the Lord? (2 Samuel 12: 9). We as South Africans, have despised the righteousness of God.

However it was because of God's grace that Jesus Christ was crucified precisely for us to repent and be reconciled with Him, whom we have rejected. South Africans, lets repent. God will forgive us.

Resuming our discussion on TRC: we will have blacks attacking whites and whites attacking blacks but we dare not generalise. Let's treat crime as it unfolds and stop assuming that all whites or all blacks are like the criminal apprehended. Mandela once said after the assassination of Chris Hani. 'A white person has killed a black person; but a white person has helped the police apprehend that white person. If you say white people must be killed for this, which white person are you going to kill'?

Difficult as it is, we need to go past the perception of seeing crime through the eye blinded by colour.

Secondly, we need to appreciate the sincerity of the Codesa, (Convention for a Democratic South Africa) negotiations. This was a negotiating forum set up by the then South African government and the eighteen other political organizations. The result was the signing of the National Peace Accord. When Mandela and the ANC team agreed to land expropriation with compensation, it was because the Treasury was overflowing with money. As soon as Mandela disappeared from these shores our enormously educated black brothers and sisters that we normally refer to as CEO's and some cadres, in charge of State Owned Entities, gave that money to an Indian family. Thereby swapping a white monopoly capital with an India monopoly capital. Corruption, crime and maladministration became the order of the day. Particularly in the period between 2007 and 2017. That money is now finished our opposition parties, PAC, BFLFand EFF, are wooing votes to themselves by accusing Nelson Mandela of having sold the struggle. Check your facts.

None of those implicated in this corruption have come-out to acknowledge wrong doing. All we as citizens were left with is denial. As we grow in Christ, we learn to own our transgressions and aspire to address them. In Christian language it is referred to as confession of sins. It is paramount to everyone and every nation to know that this world and all in it, belong to God, (Psalm 24: 1) and that same God has a Son called Jesus Christ, "who will Judge the World in the end of times,"(1 Peter 4:5).

The psalmist, above, tell us that rulers or presidents govern on behalf of God. If one goes through the many chapters of the two books of 'Kings' in the Bible, all the kings that reigned in Israel were chosen to fulfil God instructions or God's righteousness. A common proclamation underpins the choice and inauguration of every king, in those books and that is "He either did what was good or bad in the eyes of God", and this determined his fate. This is prudent as we are merely mortals and are apt to sin and fall. Solomon was imbued with wisdom, but as mortal sinner, he forgot the first wisdom principle, and that is "To fear the Lord", (Proverbs 9: 10).

Interestingly, the book of Proverbs was written by the very Solomon who defied God, (1 Kings 11: 1-12). The reader should note that it is tempting to conclude that the heathen women Solomon married were the cause of his sins against God. I differ vehemently and say that the God given wisdom should have seen him doing far better. This leads us to the observation that when leaders walk without God's guidance, they end up making empty promises and wrong decisions, the hallmark of South African politicians.

Jesus deals with this hypocrisy, (Matthew 23: 3) when he warns against the teachers of the law and Pharisees, "Do what they tell you to do but do not do what they do, for they do not practice what they preach". The entire chapter 23 deals with this insincerity.

4

The Impact of a 'Legal Crime.'

"Yet you have turned justice into gall."

Amos 6: 12

This phenomenon of legal crime, reared its 'entire' head since the dawn of former President Jacob Zuma's tenure. I use the word entire because there are indications that the arms deal corruption case that was dismissed with no one being held accountable, will now be re-opened and some insinuations are that some ministers in the Thabo Mbeki administration were also involved.

The concept of a legal crime seems contradictory and ludicrous. However it is a reality and a source of corruption and its twin sister, crime. To the best of my ability, it happens only in South Africa. Legal crime is exactly what its name suggest, a crime that is legal.

To commit this kind of crime you need to have protective constitutional rights and for the courts to deal with the culprit, they will first have to navigate through these rights. An outstanding example of this kind of crime played itself out at the Constitutional Court when all Opposition parties sought help for the removal of former president Jacob

Zuma. A big chunk of the South African public also took to the streets shouting 'Zuma must fall.' He was accused of 'unduly benefitting from Nkandla renovations'. In tandem, the concept of 'State Capture' was strongly suspected.

This phrase, 'unduly benefitting' in normal terms is theft. The first trick is that when applied to the President, it is called unduly benefitting and when it is applied to an ordinary South African, it is called theft. The second trick is that there is no court designed to deal with 'a legal crime,' because all courts are designed and intended to deal with crime. As a result the logical court that could deal with this crime is the Constitutional Court, by virtue of it having the power to interpret the Constitution. A principle of equality before the Law was grossly violated.

This because when an ordinary citizen is caught at her/his place of residence, with stolen goods, she/he is arrested on the spot. To rebuff the accusation of complicity, the citizen needs to report to the Police if somebody delivers goods that were not ordered or is doing work at the property that he/she did not request. Jacob Zuma did none of the reporting but the police could not arrest him because he was the President, with enormous rights. When the South African Constitution was drafted, it was not foreseen that a president could steal, hence no provision was made to refer the President directly to the Criminal Court. A loophole exploited to the hilt by the Guptas.

However even there, in the Constitutional Court, the attempt to impeach Jacob Zuma for violating his oath of office, was shown to be impossible. It could be gleaned from the Chief Justice as he persistently asked the Advocate representing the Opposition Parties, "How may I help you"? What the Chief Justice was highlighting was the very fact that this is a legal crime; although there is theft involved, the institution that is best suited to deal with it is not the Courts of Law, but the Cabinet.

Now the Cabinet does not use statue laws to assess a crime. It uses some self-imposed yardsticks, such as the rights and popularity of the person involved, in this case the President. The famous statement by then Free State Premier, Ace Magashule, reverberated throughout South Africa, 'The President was voted to lead and he will have to be voted out at the party conference.' Then comes the jig-saw puzzle: those who need to vote him out, were themselves appointed by him, the President, and the 'pay back clause' springs into action. Maybe we should use a relevant clause, 'you can't hit the hand that once fed you; I rendered you a favour, by appointing you to Cabinet and its now your time to return that favour'. You then come up with a street-verdict that was an extension of the above by Magashule, '… those who want to re-move him, are hell-bend on regime change and are agents of white monopoly capital.' This in spite of the crime that Jacob Zuma had com-mitted. Then Ace Magashule, went a step further and coined a phrase, 'Hands-of/off-Zuma.'

When Chief Justice Mogoeng Mogoeng, was swearing in Ministers after the election of the President Cyril Ramaphosa, he first gave them a tongue lashing regarding honesty towards the Constitution of the Re-public, (The Star February 28 2018). The Chief Justice was actually re-emphasising the fact that the Courts of Law are incapable of dealing with 'legal crime'. So you guys, (Ministers) need to have your con-science or common sense sharpened at all times.

However it was discovered that this cancer of legal crime had spread to the looting of the Treasury and the SOE, (State Owned En-tities) in pursuance of enriching an Indian family, the Guptas. To quote the Bible, "These are sensual people who cause division, who are con-trolled by their natural desires" (Jude 1: 19). If Jesus Christ was The Lord and Saviour of this family, they would have had second thoughts before causing the resultant misery to the ever-trusting-South African community. It is estimated by News 24 that this family looted well over R40 billion from state coffers. This brings us to delve into the reasons for the establishment of the South African Constitutional Court.

The Reasons behind the formation of the Constitutional Court

Truth be told, when the South African Constitution was drafted in the nineties, by intellectual giants like Nelson Mandela and Cyril Ramaphosa, nobody realised that the country will be faced with such lack of foresight that the Guptas are now exploiting. We all remember that we as the South African public, were afforded an opportunity to comment, criticize and make amendments before it was adopted. It was precisely for this reason that The Constitutional Court was incepted, by Nelson Mandela, 'to pluck the loopholes that were not evident in its drafting', (Speech by Nelson Mandela at the inauguration of the Constitutional Court, 14 February 1995). (www.anc.org/content /speech-president. 14 May 2018). This document is attached at the back of this book for reference.

What comes out very clearly in Nelson Mandela speech is the details of the minutes dealing with the mandate of this court in that meeting behind closed doors with the Judges. The reason is not far to gather, very few of the people of South Africa knew about such a Court.

Before we indulge the Constitutional Court in something that probably has nothing to do with their mandate we need to peruse the motivation behind its inception. The document on South African History on-line gives us a clearer picture of what was on Nelson Mandela's mind when he spearheaded the formation of this Court. "The notion of a bill of rights for South Africa can be traced to an ANC document in the early 1920s. The Freedom Charter of 1955 carried the idea forward. In the following decades the idea of an entrenched bill of rights received much support from liberal academics and Judges.

The crucial question was who will enforce it. The answer was provided by the Constitutional Committee of the ANC in 1991 where it was concluded that the Constitutional Court in a hybrid continental form such as that of Germany: which is able to hear cases by direct access , as well as by referral and on appeal," (https://www.concourt .org.za>about-us).

I have highlighted the word enforce because in the mind of Nelson Mandela and by experience from apartheid era, the courts were used to erode peoples' rights on the basis of flimsy reasons such as one nation being superior than the other. As a result the phrase 'enforce by direct access's was used in the connotation that the Court does not necessarily have to wait for the issue to be brought to its attention. Merely being aware that somebody or some peoples' rights have been infringed, the Court was mandated to intervene. Perhaps some valid examples need to be highlighted here. When the car of Jacob Zuma son, Duduzane, was involved in a collision with a taxi and two people lost their lives, by constitutional right that ensures all are equal before the law, he should have been charged. Therefore when the National Prosecuting Authority, (NPA), refused to charge him, the Constitutional Court should have intervened and called the NPA to order.

An inquest court, which was in my mind, completely unnecessary had the Constitutional Court done what it agreed it would do, came to a finding that indeed Duduzane Zuma needs to stand trial. Still the NPA refused to charge him. Again by word and agreement reached with the Constitutional Committee of the ANC in 1991, the Court should have intervened to call the NPA to order.

The second example is the infringement of the rights of the lady that was denied a hearing in the court when Grace Mugabe, the wife of the then Zimbabwean President, assaulted her. The government granted her diplomatic immunity, almost immediately. This was overturned in a subsequent court case where the Judge ruled it was unconstitutional for Grace to be protected by the government. In short the government was called to order not to intervene on issues that are beyond their constitutional mandate. This ruling should have been enforced by the Constitutional Court based on the agreement with the ANC committee in 1991. Surprisingly, it was through the intervention of Afri-Forum that the two cases were dealt with constitutionally. Coming closer home, let's consider the banks actions against the Guptas looting our money.

The Standard Bank Evidence in the Zondo Commission of Inquiry.

Thirdly, the Constitutional Court as agreed, needs to be decisive on the grounds of a damaging rumour. This fact is revealed in Mandela speech at the inauguration of this Court, when he says, 'the world over, governments do involve special institutions', (Line 29-30) to curb unconstitutional behaviour. It was not clear, at least for a man in the street like myself, what he meant by the functions of the special institutions, until the banking sector was called before the Zondo Commission to answer why they decided to close the Gupta accounts. Ian Sinton came to our rescue when he stated they did this based on the rumour that the Guptas were involved in money laundering. First to close the accounts was the Absa bank and Standard bank, decided to follow suit, based on the fact that they were governed by the same rules as Absa bank.

It sounds bizarre that a court can be called upon to act on a rumour. But, according to Ian Sinton, in response to the inquiry by the then Secretary General of the ANC Gwede Mantashe regarding the termination of the Gupta accounts, they had to, (Page 136-141 of Standard Bank evidence at the Zondo Commission of Inquiry).

Sinton identifies some key phases that can be called a call to the Constitutional Court, 'our version of the special institution' to act. One is Know Your Client, (KYC). The second is Politically Exposed Persons, (PEP). On page 139 of his testimony, he goes on to single out two statutes that are relevant to good relations between the bank and client namely, Financial Intelligence Centre Act, (FICA) and the Prevention and Combating of Corrupt Activities Act, (PCCAA). Point (d) states "Fica obliges all financial institutions to (i) undertake KYC, procedures before establishing any new relationship with a customer (ii) undertake enhanced due diligence if the KYC indicates that any PEP's have influence over the customer (iii) monitor every customer's transactions to understand the source and application of all funds and (iv) report any suspicious transactions to the Financial Intelligence Centre." Point (h) of the evidence by Standard Bank states that to avoid prosecution under FICA the best thing to do is to terminate the relationship with the customer if the suspicion of KYC and PEP is suspected.

Because of ignoring the stipulations of KYC and PEP above, Standard Bank Tanzania was fined US$38m for ignoring to act on a rumour and they did not want a repetition of that incident in South Africa. The reader should please note that there was no documentary proof that the client Standard Bank assisted to gain a lucrative government contract in Tanzania was politically connected. It was just an advice from USA regarding the danger of dealing with the tainted client that landed Standard Bank this hefty fine. Our special institution, the Constitutional Court of South Africa, was given an opportunity to deal with a politically tainted Guptas through Jacob Zuma and it gave us an unimpressive result.

The three incidents above give impetus to the words Nelson Mandela used in his speech. Particularly the last point mentioned because a rumour was already doing rounds that crime and corruption in South Africa had its origin from the highest office in South Africa, the office of the then President Jacob Zuma.

When the Constitutional Court was called upon to adjudicate on the Zuma corruption, it is accepted, by virtue of them being a special institution that they already knew even before the evidence of the opposition parties was presented before it that Jacob Zuma was engaged on shoddy dealings. Secondly they also knew about the Guptas being Politically Exposed Persons. This information they should have collected on their own and not wait to be fed it like in an ordinary court of law, that's what a special institution is tasked with, following Sinton's evidence.

In that speech Mandela, used lyrics which can be rightly be regarded as prophecy, he said "Today I rise…to inaugurate a court South Africa never had, a court on which hinges the future of our democracy….attacks on human rights being couched in innocent language, (line 18-19). The two statements, 'it is the task of this Court to ensure that the values of freedom and equality line…and Parliament will never attempt to pass laws, Line 24 can be rightly interpreted as Mandela referring to this Court and Parliament never to turn a blind eye on the source of corruption…are nurtured and protected… We expect you to be creative, line 45"

In closing his speech Mandela said, "In the end you have only the Constitution and your conscience, line 91, on which you can rely. We look upon you to serve both without fear or favour".

I nearly collapsed when I read the convicting statements 'and use your conscience.' This is in contradiction to 'ANC conscience' during Jacob Zuma era. My view has always been that the phrase, 'Your conscience' is an Opposition Parties' invention, that it applied to ANC MP's only and that it never applied to the Constitutional Court. I am baffled!

In addition, the narrative that the ANC derives its life from the 'ANC Conscience' as former president Zuma has made the world to believe, is clearly a deviation from the Mandela ANC, that used 'individual conscience', as a result that is plagiarism. We now have a Zuma ANC usurped from a Mandela ANC. Plagiarism is a punishable offence, had it not been for the concept of a 'legal crime'.

So, back to the court, when the defence advocate was confronted with the question from the Chief Justice, 'How may I help you', he should have said, be creative and use your conscience like you people agreed in your discussions of the formation of this Court with Nelson Mandela. Out of respect, which I fully agree with, he withheld the comment.

Nelson Mandela, used his conscience, remember the 'do it first principle,' much to the chagrin of the entire ANC, when the then rugby head, Louis Luyt hauled him before the court. Then, before entering the Court, Nelson Mandela said to the reporters, "I have to go to the Court, to show that nobody including the President is above the Law".

Inside the court, a visibly livid Mandela, because he was being belittled by the rugby man said, "I am attending this case out of respect for the administration of justice" (www.independent.co.uk/news/rugby-boss-forces-mandela -into -court. 1151248.html. 07.05.2018).

'Respect for the administration of justice' is Jesus Christ's teaching on righteousness or justness.

Now compare a Mandela who was merely despised but did attend court, to a Zuma that was accused of theft but could not be convicted because of the legal crime. Add to this the Cabinet that was not even considering the option of removing him, because they were using the ANC conscience, not theirs. It was then clear that Zuma will be president for as long as his term of office was in effect. This despite the ravages he was causing to the economy.

Then lightning struck!

By this time Jacob Zuma had already expelled the Minister of Finance, Nhlanhla Nene and replaced him with Des van Rooyen. Something the economic markets began to cast aspersions to. The clouds were gathering! And disaster was about to strike!

Jacob Zuma in response to the advice of the economic turbulence this was causing, removed van Rooyen and replaced him with Pravin Gordhan. Then word came out that Gordhan had to answer plus minus 27 questions from Tom Moyane regarding SARS rogue unit and the tension, which was brewing, between Pravin Gordhan, and Jacob Zuma. By this time, the economic growth that Zuma inherited from Thabo Mbeki at 4%, was at the brink of junk status and there was no respite in sight.

Some background is necessary here; I pensioned on 1 April 2015, after working thirty-five years at Nampak Ltd, Vanderbijl Park. When you receive your old age pension from your employer, one thing rings in your skull, 'this is your last pay packet, use it wisely'. Use it wisely, means invest and only use the interest from investment, steer away from touching your capital, popularly known as lump sum. That's exactly what I did. For this transaction to be effected, one has to forfeit 0.0325% of one's investment to the financial advisor. It is an insignificant amount if markets are doing well, as they were in 2015 and a catastrophe if there is a disturbance in the economy.

My investment was doing very well for the first 8 months. Then disaster struck! I still remember, vividly, when my financial advisor called me in 2016 and said; 'This is urgent, you need to come so as to reconsider this investment otherwise by the time you come back here, you won't be having money, because it is being eroded', Markets are not performing. By this time it had lost 10% of its value. I learnt then that the economy of the country is by itself an employer. Ever wondered why South Africa has so many immigrants and foreign nationals, the economy here is performing better than most African countries and the world.

If markets do well, you can go draw some money from your unit trusts and have food on the table for your family. Otherwise you go on an unplanned and undeserved hunger strike. The catastrophe was correctly explained by Mcebisi Jonas at the Zondo Commission of Inquiry in August 2018. It was like he was stating my case.

President Cyril Ramaphosa wants to grow the economy that means he wants to grow this 'employer' to fight poverty!

The only way to save guard my investment was to put it in a fixed deposit for at least five years. To rub salt into an open wound, a pensioner who has an investment, like myself, by government decree, according to what Sassa told me, does not qualify for a grant. People normally say there is no such thing as a stupid question but I recalled asking the financial advisor a very stupid question, "In your sessions about investments, do you people sometimes involve Judges, so that they are aware of the incredulous assault crime and corruption cause on the economy?" The answer was, we don't, because they know!

When I left the financial advisor's office, to my luck, I was alone and this gave me a chance to take a turn into the public commodes to shed a tear. It was unbelievable! When I pensioned in March 2015, the investment world looked so promising, by the time Pravin Gordhan was expelled in the middle of the night in 2017, my world had turned upside down. It is only by God's grace that those who are on pension like myself are surviving, and I know there were many who were adversely affected by Jacob Zuma's merciless decisions.

To those I say, although we may cry, Eloi, Eloi, lama sabachtani, (Mark 15: 34 this leads us back to Him who is faithful, "Come to me you who are weary and heavy laden and I will give you rest" (Matthew 11: 28)

As the Chief Justice sent the opposition parties packing back to Parliament to solve their problem, it flashed on me the reason why Nelson Mandela first introduced the idea of establishing a Constitutional Court, "To help where a confusion arises regarding a constitutional matter".

Meanwhile I was grappling with fact that Judges of the Constitutional Court do not reside in Tristandacuna, an island somewhere in the wilderness beyond Cape Town. They must have heard on the media or read newspapers some of the comments made by high ranking officials of the ANC that have adversely influenced its conscience from what Nelson Mandela moulded it.

Firstly, I remembered a lady that was once the Minister of Communications, Faith Muthambi. At some point she had to expel an incompetent and under qualified COO of the SABC. She was dragging her feet or to put it in the right context; she stated it bluntly that she was not about to fire this culprit because, as the Newspapers reported, "U baba u yamthanda". Now this ubaba was former President Zuma who was allegedly a friend of this man. In short what Ms Faith Muthambi was saying is, if you want to hurt Zuma, don't come to me, try next door, worst still if you want expel him! Do not count on me! When opposition parties headed back to Parliament to argue their case, they were already minus one vote by virtue of Muthambi's unwavering loyalty to Zuma.

Secondly, it turned out that the entire ANC MPs' were mummified and ordered to vote according to party line and not along their conscience, a Mandela hall-mark. This was garnered from both the then ANC Secretary General Gwede Mantashe and Chief Whip Jackson Mthembu who stated on numerous occasions that 'no army commander; the army commander being Jacob Zuma, would allow his subjects to fight the battle for the opposition'. This was a clear cry of dereliction by the two gentlemen that ANC members of the Cabinet are dictated to on how to vote on motions of no confidence by the very person they must vote out. Indeed after a number of 'No confidence votes' against Zuma, the ANC was known to vote hundred percent against the motion. I believe this was a miracle by all world standards. I'm still wondering whether it has ever happened anywhere in the world that 240 people will on numerous occasions, vote hundred percent in favour of one thing. It must definitely be included in the Genius Book of Records.

When God sent Prophet Ezekiel, He said, "Mortal man I am sending you to the children of Israel, to a rebellious nation that has rebelled against Me; they are stubborn…but do not be afraid… whether they listen or not…you will tell them, thus says the Lord. Whether they hear or not, but they will know a prophet was among them" (Ezekiel 2: 3-7). When people proclaim God to the public, they need to be brave and tell it is like it is.

While I was pondering on what was behind Nelson Mandela's mind to motivate the idea of a Constitutional Court, the Muthambi issue and the ANC mind set, versus the individual mind-set, I revisited his speech. Specifically looking for how Mandela could swindle the entire nation. That no one realised that this thing of the Constitutional Court will never work. Therein I came across some appealing phrases, "A court South Africa never had…be Creative…use your conscience… crime being hidden in innocent language…your tasks are new…your powers are new…finding a new way…last but not least, he said… The success of the Constitutional Court will depend to a large measure on the successful functioning of the ordinary courts."

All these words made me realise that this old-man was indeed a prophet, he played his cards openly. The Constitutional Court does not have to rely solely on law books and encyclopaedias to formulate a verdict. Because they are dealing primarily with the context of the society;

what is going on in the community, and this being South Africa, crime and corruption emanating from the head of government. This invariably requires them to apply their minds.

When Paul wrote the book of Romans he realised that he can never transform the Romans to Jesus Christ unless he went against what drives their political, social and economic life, the Law. As a result he criticised their adherence to observing the law that held Julius Caesar in high esteem, rather than God in Jesus Christ through the Holy Spirit. In South Africa, crime and corruption has become our god. To the Romans, the law included The Ten Commandments, the law of the Roman Empire and their culture, like circumcision. We may also remember when Jesus said, give unto Caesar what belongs to Caesar, (Mathew 22: 21).

The law was in turn used to determine a person's Christianity, (Romans 7). A South African metaphor is being 'political connected'. To achieve the same feat, Paul highlighted God's Grace. The hint by Mandela that crime is sometimes hidden in innocent language is exactly what happens in the South African courts. The root cause is the craftiness of the criminals who ensured they tame the Highest Court. This would ensure the lower courts are rendered powerless and have to toe the line. The heart breaking part is that Mandela envisaged the problems coming from the lower and not the highest Court.

This has to do with the legal crime. The Constitutional Court was tasked to deal with cases that could not be resolved by the smaller courts especially incidents that call into question their constitutionality. In this instance, it was vice versa, because of the legal crime concept. The lower courts could not function properly because the senior court was not successful in dealing with the man who is the source of not only legal-crime, but crime and corruption in general, Jacob Zuma.

The envisaged debate in Parliament was cut short when the then Secretary General of the ANC, Gwede Mantashe, appeared to address the media and the public, on the Nkandla outcome, and commented "The Judge did not say we should fire President Zuma". He was followed shortly thereafter by Jacob Zuma himself who apologised to the South African public and left the podium. I thought I was watching a ferry-tale movie. It reminded me of a Scripture in the Bible about a road that is so clear that nobody will ever get lost when travelling on it, (Isaiah 35: 8, JC Maxwell Bible).

Personally and I believe most South Africans and the world believed, the court would say something like "based on what Zuma has done, you, as Cabinet, need to vote him out or fire him, it's an order of this court". Remember the extra powers Mandela mentioned. The country lost an opportunity and valuable time to engage and investigate allegations of State Capture that Advocate Thuli Madonsela so passionately unearthed. I cannot imagine the frustration she is going through now.

In his speech Nelson Mandela mentioned that the world never runs short of rubber stamps, lines 43-45? What the Constitutional Court did was to rubber stamp the obvious resolution of the entire 240 ANC members of Parliament.

We now have to rely on leaked e-mails which are for that matter very questionable because even the Hawks were paralysed to motionlessness. They were dormant, while Advocate Thuli Madonsela was yearning for support. It is only now, after the removal of Jacob Zuma and election of Honourable President Cyril Ramaphosa, that they, the Hawks, sprang into action.

It is logical to assume that all the evidence leading to corruption, especially the Estina Dairy scandal and State Capture was afforded an opportunity to be erased or diluted. The 'not guilty verdicts' that emanate from the lower courts now is therefore not baffling at all, seeing that the main culprit has been let off the hook. In the Estina Dairy issue,

R250m that was meant for black emerging farmers has vanished into thin air and surprisingly, nobody has done anything wrong.

Not only that, alarm bells were ringing for Jacob Zuma and those in cahoots with him, that unless he acts quickly to find a suitable replacement that will sweep all corruption under the carpet, when he leaves office, hell is going to fly loose. It is therefore not surprising that the ANC Constitution was harassed and manipulated to make room for Nkosazana Dlamaini Zuma to succeed him. Not only that, Zuma vacated his office asking what he has done wrong. He left office threatening to return, and it looks like what he was saying will indeed materialise, unless South Africans stand firm behind Ramaphosa to see his term running to the end.

The inactivity of the ANC and the Hawks against Jacob Zuma, reminded me of Jesus Christ's Sermon on the Mount, "Blessed are those who are persecuted for righteousness' sake, for theirs is the Kingdom of Heaven" Matthew 5: 10. Righteousness will sometimes breed ones' suffering. 'The do it first' principle of Jesus Christ plays itself out here. In South Africa, by virtue of the inaction of the Constitutional Court, it is the poor masses that can rather suffer, not the leaders.

Nelson Mandela emphasised not only Encyclopaedias and Law Books in making rulings, but, in addition a 'person's conscience' in the inception of the Constitutional Court. If they felt a court cannot do without hard-core-facts, it would have been prudent of them to have declined the appointment to this Court or better still refused that a court should be used as a special institution. Remember Nelson Mandela was himself not a Judge.

Advocate Thuli Madonsela, the newly anointed prophetess, remarked sometime after her term of office ended that the longer we wait, and do not start with investigations, the more we stand to lose valuable information that can actually threaten the authenticity of the investigations and prosecutions. Not long after our prophetess said this, her prophesy was revealed. On the 9 March 2018, the High Court in Bloemfontein upheld Mr Atul Gupta's application to unfreeze his 10 Million Rand that was de-activated by the Hawks. This could have been avoided had the Constitutional Court done what every institution, banks in particular, do if somebody is suspected of dishonesty.

The usual procedure is for the person to be put on indefinite leave and if after investigations, nothing unto-ward is discovered the suspect is re-instated with the necessary compensation. Simple as that.

The Book of Romans says, "But we know that the Judgement of God is according to truth against those who practice such things", (Rom 2: 2). If God judges according to the truth, how much more should we mortals do the same.

The sad story is that what Zuma was accused of, illegal Nkandla renovations using state money, is actually theft as I stated above. It goes without saying that if theft a criminal act, is diluted as 'breaking an oath of office' when committed by the president and treated as theft when committed by ordinary citizens, there is definitely no equality before the Law. For justness of Christ to prevail, either all criminal cases are handled by the Constitutional Court as it did to Jacob Zuma or they all go to Criminal Court as all criminal cases should.

5

Some important observations from the said Mandela speech.

By this time we all agree that the Constitutional Court is a Nelson Mandela invention. By the same token, as we all know, the ANC is also a Mandela invention, (He walked from door to door canvassing people to join).

Both institutions were grounded, primarily on the understanding that those who run them, will above all, first and foremost, use the knowledge of right or wrong in upholding the Rule of Law.

The role of Christ in leadership as emphasised by Paul:

St Paul stopped at nothing to warn people and leaders in particular, to walk with Christ in all they do, "I therefore, prisoner of the Lord, beseech you that you walk worthy of the vocation wherewith ye are called" (Ephesians 4: 1 JCM Bible).

Paul and Peter highlight an important invigorator, The Holy Spirit, by which good leadership can be practised.

In Romans 8: 12-17, Paul again says, "Bretheren, we are debtors not to flesh…v15, for you did not receive the spirit of bondage again to fear…you received the Spirit of adoption by whom you cry Abba, Father…by this Spirit we are children of God…that we may also be glorified together"

1 Peter 1: 11, goes further, "…This was the time to which Christ Spirit in them was pointing in predicting the sufferings that Christ would have to endure…"

Therefore the process of salvation and righteousness is not complete until one embraces the Holy Spirit which is in the world now. Jesus Christ, paving the advent of the Holy Spirit said, "This Spirit will teach you all things," John 14: 25.' Teach you all things' including how to transform a corrupt and crime infested country like South Africa, to a peaceful, God loving one. In verse 14 of the same chapter, Jesus Christ promises that He and the Father will reside in anybody who loves Him. When God resides in you, you can't commit a sin better known as corruption.

The reader must have realised that the Bible deals with Triune God, The Father, Jesus Christ and the Holy Spirit which is referred to as the Holy Trinity. It is not stated as Trinity in the Bible, but it is there as can be seen in the foregoing discussion. The heresies that emanated from the detractors of the early Church regarding the notion of Trinity, resulted in the formulation of the three creeds by the Christian Church namely, the Nicene, Apostles' and Athanasian Creeds. Which are never-the-less not the subject of this book. I am just mentioning it to advise our government that wisdom is just a prayer away.

The Role of the ANCWL:

I have already touched on the part played by this league when I discussed Nkosazana Dlamini Zuma, and her being thrust in the deep end by Jacob Zuma, her former husband. The actions of the NPA regarding possible prosecution of her son Duduzane, in the death of Dube reveal without doubt why former President Zuma so anxiously wanted her to be the next President. We may argue until the end of times that it is her competency that was behind that move, but doubt will forever be there that the contrary is the case.

The fact that numerous commissions of inquiry are in session is by no shred of doubt only because of Cyril Ramaphosa being the President of the country. Had Nkosazana Dlamini Zuma been at this hot seat it is unthinkable that she would have pursued this route knowing fully well that her son may end up in jail. It is only worth noting that it was only through the Presidency of Cyril that charges against Duduzane Zuma regarding the car accident, were pushed through by Afri-Forum, something that was stunted during Jacob Zuma's Presidency.

As a member of the ANCWLeague, I believe she should have refused to be dragged from not being a Member of Parliament to a position where she found herself competing for the position of the President of the ANC. Tradition and not policy of the ANC has all along been that the Deputy President becomes the President when the latter's term of office comes to an end. I believe the ANCWL should have argued for the appointment of a woman who was already in Parliament. Unfortunately the League, just like Jacob Zuma, wanted the woman and not a woman.

The convenient tacit approval, by the ANCWL, poses a serious threat to the integrity, rights and dignity of women folk. Her preference by Jacob Zuma can correctly be perceived as nepotism, a huge scourge within the ANC.

In the same breath, I expected the League to reprimand Advocate Busisiwe Mkhwebane or going a step further to demand she steps down, because of her incompetence. Advocate Thuli Madonsela handed her the baton to vigorously pursue State Capture inquiry. Instead she embarked on a ridiculous task to change the mandate of the Reserve Bank, something that has nothing to do with the job she was mandated to do. To make matters worse she even lost the court case with costs for the same course. To think that Judges are selected from Advocates and here we have an Advocate who still battles to formulate a winnable case, or understanding how a mandate looks like. Small wonder the R250million in Estina meant for emerging farmers in Vrede is missing and no one can be held accountable. Surprisingly, because according to her, Ace Magashule is not implicated. Meaning it would only have been an offence if the former Free State Premier was implicated.

Furthermore, why did the ANCWL not vigorously recommend that a woman, Advocate Thuli Madonsela complete her outstanding piece of work on State Capture before handing over to Advocate Busisiwe Mkhwebane, is a question that will haunt South Africans for ages to come. Our first Public Protector, Selby Baqwa was asked, by government, to extend his term of office and he declined. It would not have been a new initiative to do the same with Advocate Thuli Madonsela.

The Guptas who are alleged to have benefitted immensely from the project are laughing at the ignorance of our law enforcement officers.

We have had women in the past ten years during Jacob Zuma's term in office who were doing badly in government and the League never raised an ire of concern.

Be that as it may, the last thing we can do is to generalise that women are incompetent. Since the dawn of the fight against apartheid there has always been women who did outstanding work. In fact leadership in our corporate world is filled with people of both sexes.

As a matter of fact, Jesus Christ demonstrated that women are born leaders: The woman at the well, (John 4: 28-30) transformed the entire city without having received the Holy Spirit like the disciples, (Matthew 28: 19). An adulterous woman was taken to Jesus as a piece of rubbish by men and women who held themselves in high esteem. She was cleansed and returned to the township empowered to transform her detractors, (John 8: 1-12). In John 20, Mary was the first to announce

Jesus' resurrection when His disciples, men, were in hiding. Mary went to the grave early in the morning when it was still dark, alone. I challenge any man to go to the graveyard alone, at that hour, close your eyes and say Our Father, if you can do it for 1 minute without opening your eyes, you are tough. I once tried it, because I did not believe a woman can beat me and I could not close my eyes…thinking about the ghosts. I even saw one which wanted to squeeze my last breath out!!!

This shows the immense potential bestowed on women by Jesus Christ. This is a clear indication that they cannot be undermined at will by men. You may recall that God treated Rebecca and Isaac, her husband, as equal.

It is on this note that I want to plead with Nkosazana Dlamini Zuma, to steer clear of the position of President of the country. Those implicated in corruption are doing everything to change the constitution even that of the ANC, so that corruption can fester more. Let Cyril be the leader until at least 2024 for corruption to be uprooted in South Africa. Jesus Christ be with you!

I also want to appeal to all and sundry to desist from supporting corruption by doing everything to get rotten potatoes back in our government. Ace Magashule announced recently in KZN that they only need five years to return to corruption.

I want to appeal to captains of industries that should this be the case, please do not pay tax. Collect it and save it until corruption is no more. The unfortunate part is that the very people who vote corrupt leaders to lead are the once who will suffer most. Secondly, our courts are being used to fester crime, we can't get to the bottom of this scourge because of the pre-determined prosecutorial decisions. Drug lords are arrested and in no time roam the streets, cash in transit heists happen at an alarming rate and there is no solution in sight. This brings us to the question, 'Is it not time to pension all judges, close all the courts of law and let it be a-free-for-all-country?'

6

Zuma considering another appeal:

On 18 March 2018, eNCA reported on the news that Jacob Zuma is considering to appeal the decision by Shaun Abrahams to prosecute him. Whether this appeal will indeed go ahead, is in my mind, immaterial. The pertinent question is, so many appeals by a man who was, for the nine years, the custodian of our constitution? Not only that, he was also directly involved in the appointment of some of these Judges, the efficiency of which he is now casting aspersions to.

I wish to bring to the reader's attention that Jacob Zuma's application to have this case thrown out of court has been dismissed. A trial is in the offing. This thanks to the organization called Corruption Watch.

Subsequently a number of questions come to mind:

For him and his surrogates to question the fairness of his trial, means the man does not have faith in the judicial system, of which he was a custodian. Why then should we, as ordinary South Africans not doubt it?

Secondly with so many Judges in agreement that he should be prosecuted, which Judge is he head hunting that will hold a different view and why does he hold that believe? The NPA which has to prepare the case against Zuma, is still of the view, like Mokotedi Mpshe who squashed the charges in the first indictment, that he should not stand trial. Should South Africans then believe they will see justice done? Mokotedi Mpshe is now a Judge and one can justly imagine the outcome of the trial should he be the presiding Judge in this case. Will he overrule his earlier verdict? Will the NPA prepare a water tight case against their initial no-case-to-answer resolution? It remains to be seen.

In the much anticipated trial of Duduzane Zuma, which he won, it was the very NPA that refused to charge him initially, that had to prepare a case against him.

Recently the NPA had to appeal, twice, a verdict of culpable homicide, until a six year jail term was converted to fifteen years. One can correctly say this is one case that the NPA out deed itself.

In this twice appealed case, I wish to state categorically that had the Court taken into account the evidence presented by the fabulous Captain Chris Mangena, it would not have been necessary to even go for the appeal, let alone twice. In analysing the sequence of the bullets, Captain Chris Mangena proved beyond doubt that it was the victim that was crying in the morning of the incident and not the perpetrator.

Most importantly, shouldn't everybody facing a criminal trial be afforded the same opportunity of so many appeals, like Zuma, paid by the State? Since it now appears our Judges are incapable of executing a fair trial? The Daily Maverick, Saturday 29 June 2019, discuss this issue at length under the heading, "Money is the unfair advantage in the business of using law to seek justice."

Secondly, the many supporters that will follow Zuma to Court, what influence can they have this time around, considering the bizarre verdict in the Khwezi rape trial? In that instance the victim was sent packing to some faraway place, while the alleged offender, instead of going to jail for 15 or 25 years, was afforded an opportunity to be the President of the country. Who then is the biggest loser in such situations, the victim or the criminal justice system? The perception among the Zuma supporters is that he is being targeted by some dark forces who want his and the ANC downfall.

Touching on the Khwezi case, one cannot resist the urge to call into question the credibility of the ANCWL. While Jacob Zuma ascended the throne to be President of the country, this lady was left at the mercy of the very Zuma she was accusing. The South African embassy is the direct link between a citizen and the country. The embassy works through the President of the country. Could it be that this lady had to secure her daily meal by pleading the embassy which in turn had to contact the President to augment the daily allowance? Was the League not obliged to come to her rescue, seeing that she lost her case? Why was it still necessary to send her into exile?

The Church of Christ

Surprisingly, included among the different formations that cry "Zuma is being unfairly targeted" is the Church of Christ. On Good Friday, 29 March 2018, Zuma was addressing Christians on how he is falsely accused. Apparently his being 'falsely' indicted is likened to that of Jesus Christ. I observed Arch-bishops, Bishops and the entire congregation clapping hands and ululating. What I expected the Church leaders in there to explain to Jacob Zuma, was that Jesus never ran a string of appeals to set his charges aside, like he is doing. If he is innocent, he needs to go to court to proof same.

Any corruption needs to be ridiculed but if it is hidden under the guise of racism, it never will be addressed.

To reconcile my comment about the Chief Justice on the 28th February, I expected the Chief Justice to say to Ministers 'Don't do what we did in the Nkandla debacle'. I will come back to this particular action of the Constitutional court when I discuss recommendations under the heading 'Conclusion' on page 101.

When you rule you rule on behalf of God, "Who is head of all principality and power" (Col 2: 10)

7

Ill-discipline at our schools:
Children become the future government.

> " But whoever causes any one of these little ones who believe in me to stumble, it would be better for him if a millstone was hung around his neck, and he were thrown in the sea"
>
> Mark 9: 42

On the 12 March 2018, a student was seen on a TV clip moving towards a teacher and throwing a book that hit her. To me she appeared too young to be that much violent. The school has line authority which includes the parents and the school governing bodies, (SGB's). That line authority should have been approached by the child and the parents to address the misunderstanding between the two, rather than the child displaying that level of aggression. One thing that emerged clearly was that relations between the child and the teacher have irrevocably been destroyed. It will take an effort between them to be restored, to the detriment of the entire class and school. Even if they are results of provocation, as was claimed, proper channels that will benefit all students was the ideal way.

The full picture of what is happening in classes was painted on page one of the New Age Newspaper, 19 March 2018, it was a comment on the previous incident. The main heading was "SA's classrooms of war", with the following sub-heading, "Teachers punching bags for pupils, traumatised teachers demand greater protection, police often summoned to restore order and attacks on teachers a tip of the iceberg".

I could only read with amazement and asked myself, 'When did this all start because up to 1974, when I finished my Matric, I had never seen, let alone heard of a situation where teachers were punching bags for students. It never happened during that time'.

Truth be told, this all started when the Constitution provided for children to be immune from punishment. I would like to draw the reader's attention to the big difference between assault/injury and punishment like using the palm of your hand.

What the Bible compels the parent and therefore the teacher to do is to effect punishment on the child for misbehaviour, Proverbs 13: 24, "He who spares his rod hates his son, but he who loves him, disciplines him promptly". The Bible states it very clearly that it is hatred if you do not punish a child. Because the Constitution of the country has encouraged this 'hatred' from the parents, the children have taken the law into their hands and in return are the ones who dish out the hatred to parents and teachers. It is very interesting that no political party has emerged to condemn this behaviour by the youth. This is obviously because they do not want to lose votes among the youth.

Remember children will initially not like you as a disciplinarian, that's how we felt when we were punished during our times. But we have come to realise it was for a good cause. Whoever came with the theory and fed it our government, that punishing a child will yield negative results, got it all wrong. She/he must be reprimanded for misleading the nation and the world. Hopefully he/she is still alive.

The fact of the matter is that some theories are only good for the book but definitely not practical and withholding punishment from a child is one such theory. It has proved to be a miserable failure and disastrous to ethical behaviour in South Africa. It needs to be removed from the Constitution.

In the scripture on this topic above, Jesus refers to children as 'the little ones who believe in Me'. Meaning children, young as they are, have a natural or divine inclination to Christ, "Let the children come to me, do not forbid them…" (Luke 18: 16). Parents and government have a divine obligation to nurture this God given talent of the children and I repeat withholding punishment is therefore a way of the devil.

In the same newspaper, it was reported that teachers are lamenting the conviction they took to make children better people. The situation is utmost hopeless and dangerous to their lives. They give avowed statements that the government has lost the battle on discipline. One teacher describes it as "A never ending traumatic experience". Another goes on and says, "Even principals are running out of ideas on how to deal with violent pupils". Interestingly it is always the pupils who are violent against the teachers and not the other way round, because teachers are by law, expelled from teaching if they are violent against students.

Raising the question, why are students not expelled when they are violent against teachers? Because our law is on the side of the oppressor. And the oppressor this time is not based on race classification but the students.

I personally hold the view that our Constitution is breeding crime!

Quoting another source; on page 7 of the City Press News Paper, 18 March 2018, there is a cry of despondence by parents, "Our Schools are getting worse". Somewhere in the middle of this article there is spine chilling finding and it goes like this, "The Global Parents Survey, commissioned in December last year, by the Varkey Foundation- a non-profit organization, established to improve the standard of education for under privileged children throughout the world, found out that almost three-quarters (72%) of South African parents think standards of education have become worse in the past ten years. This was more than any other countries surveyed.

The survey found that local parents also had the highest proportion (50%) of those who thought education had become worse in the "past ten years". The phrase "Past ten years", poses an interesting revelation because this is the term in office of Jacob Zuma. How a dozen judges of the Constitutional Court missed this state of affairs, the increasing moral decay, when the joint effort of the Opposition Parties pleaded with it, in the Nkandla saga, 'help us remove this man from office', is beyond any shred of imagination.

The notion that South Africa is a Constitutional democracy, rests among others on the principle that all people are equal before the Law and that every citizen has rights that need to be respected. This means in exercising one's rights, do not infringe on others'. A Biblical equivalent of this is love your neighbour as you love yourself. If you misuse the tax money as was evident in the mismanagement of the State Owned Enterprises', you are obviously infringing on my right to receive services out of the tax citizens pay. Small wonder the country is reverberating with riots, lack of service demonstration, the killing of police and members of the public.

The incident of a student throwing a book at a teacher has escalated into the murder of teachers. In Limpopo, a teacher was stabbed to death for reprimanding a student. As if that was not enough, another was shot dead in Kwazulu Natal. Still the Government shows no indication of providing a remedy. Say, the said teachers managed to wrestle the weapon from the student and stabbed or shot the student. A question that would open the prison doors in the court of Law for the teacher would be, 'Now that you had already neutralised the threat why did you proceed to kill the 'innocent/poor' child? It would be followed by the usual rhetoric, 'students cum criminals, go to school to be taught not murdered…we will deal with this murderer of a teacher so that we send a stern warning to those who still think they can take the law into their hands by murdering our 'poor' children. I wonder why they are always poor.

The principle of respect for life, is actually a respect for life of the potential voter, regardless of whether it's a murderer that is being protected.

As if to rub salt in an open wound, the Constitutional Court on 18 October 2019, ruled that it is a criminal offence to spank your own child. By your child I mean your own flesh and blood. While we do not have a way of apprehending and convicting truck burners, destroyers of buildings like police stations, traffic robots, (whether in service delivery protests, or acts of zenophobia) trains and cash-in-transit heisters and the accompanying loss of life, to name a few, we now know it's a criminal offence to spank your child. For spanking your child to end up in court of law, your child needs to lay a charge against you as a parent.

Psychologists that were interviewed on TV for this ruling agreed the court was spot on. 'Because, according them, spanking your child you are teaching your child to be violent.' If there was any measure of disciplining children not to be violent, we would have applied it and prevented the incremental killing of teachers at schools. This behaviour is definitely not on a decline, it is increasing. What was not explained by the court nor the experts on child rearing is, 'are you not teaching your child a destructive behaviour when it has you as parent under duress to provide for it, (child). Tomorrow when he has a girlfriend and cannot get his free supply, which he got used to from childhood, unfortunately this time he can't go to police station to demand 'what's rightfully his,' so he must kill? That's why we have increasing acts of violence against women and children, each year, certainly a new phenomenon indeed.

In another land mark ruling, the court ruled that the President must no longer fire cabinet ministers at will. To think that Jacob Zuma has been doing this for years and no one called him to order! In my mind the time has come for South Africans to assess, by vote, if we still need the Constitutional Court. I certainly believe it must go. Alternatively judges in there should rotate on a five or seven year basis. We voted it into existence when we endorsed the constitution, we certainly reserve the right to vote it out. The disaster facing South Africa is that the rulings from that court cannot be challenged in another court, because it is the highest court. Look at this, it is a judge in a commission of inquiry that ruled, with understandable reasons, that the President must fire Nomgcobo Jiba and Lawrence Mrwebi. It is the Constitutional Court that overruled this judge. A question may be asked, which judge or judges ruled in favour of maintenance of the rule of law, if the two affected individuals indeed did what it is alleged they did?

To the teachers, Police men and women as well as the general citizenry at the mercy of unruly students and criminals, I would like to quote Jesus Christ, "Peace I leave with you, my Peace I give you… not as the world gives…therefore let not your hearts be troubled or be afraid", (John 14: 27). This may sound ridiculous, seeing the avalanche of unfulfilled promises from our government. But still I say, "Do not lose heart, even though our outward man is perishing, yet the inward man is being renewed day by day", (2 Corinthians 4:16). Again the Bible says, "The God and Father of our Lord Jesus Christ…has begotten us again to a living hope through the resurrection of Jesus Christ from the dead". When this resurrected Jesus Christ promises us peace, then we know it is a concrete and unwavering peace because "He who promised is faithful", (Hebrew 10: 23; 1 Thessalonians 5: 24). With the dawn of Cyril Ramaphosa administration things look promising.

Answering our prayers, God has given us a man who rules and is inspired by the fear of that same God, Honourable Cyril Matamela Ramaphosa. He has started a long road of uprooting corruption. Ironically corruption was perpetrated by the very people we trusted, our cadres. We have been betrayed by our very own.

Back to our topic for this chapter. This skewed execution of justice is already prevalent in our society.

Those who uphold the law are on the receiving end of injustice. This trend starts from schools and plays itself out atrociously in public life. Criminals can kill people as they like and law abiding citizens can only get a scant promise from the authorities that "The law will take its course". The same dangerous game that students meet out to teachers at schools, is the same game that criminals under the protection of the law play, out in society. Unlicensed fire arms are used to kill people and the perpetrators are untraceable. Citizens retaliate with licensed fire arms, unlike criminals are identified and locked up.

We have heard so many times by our teacher friends, about students writing tests and examinations with Okapis and guns on the desk. This answers the question why the Minister of Basic Education, presently Angie Motshega, has to 'doctor' the final Matric results every time before they are published in Newspapers. While 30% and in some cases with a boost from around 25% is an acceptable passing mark, unfortunately in the employment field, the child is at an acute disadvantage as a good passing mark is the starting point of an employment process. This could account for the reason why unemployment is so rife among the South African youths, who have actually 'passed' Matric.

It is thus not far-fetched to suggest that our schools be segregated, wait, not along racial lines, but along those children who want to learn and be disciplined when they misbehave, and those who do not want to be disciplined and do not want to learn. This will be done to help those children who want to improve their careers and be employable and those who have already blown the final whistle on their careers and want to be unemployed. There is a parable that dictates: spare the rod and spoil the child. And that is true of our children today. Such children are in school to waste other pupils and the teachers' time.

Our children, like the criminals in our society know fully well that the law is on their side. Our Law dictates that you have to sweet-talk children when they misbehave. As a parent or a teacher you can't even give the child a spanking with the palm of your hand, something which cannot injure anybody but will send a message that misbehaviour is a punishable offence. Because of this pacifism, which will surely bore them to their nerves, children grow up knowing that they are protected by law and can do as they please. Small wonder that crime is a rampant feature in South Africa.

To remedy the situation, I suggest that those who lost their bread winners due to murder that could have been prevented but feared being prosecuted for killing the criminals, need to approach the courts for compensation. If the Law prohibits a citizen from killing a criminal under the guise of murder, then by implication the law undertakes to protect the citizens so that the citizens do not take the law into their own hands. Then the government needs to account why people are dying in the acts of criminality. This means the government has failed the people and needs to compensate them.

Now that's righteousness.

This brings us to the consideration of a number of interesting cases that have happened and continue to happen:

Cash-in-Transit heists and possible Scud missiles:

The incidents of Cash-in-transit heists have increased with the concomitant violence. Nowadays bombs are used to open up the cash vans and ATM machines.

Sometimes we read in newspapers about people being arrested at our borders from neighbouring countries in possession of bombs. Recently, suspicion has shifted to involvement of the army and the police.

In both occurrences, heists and ATM blasts, criminals do not care a hoot about people in the vehicle, around those vehicles and around ATM's. As long as they can retrieve what is 'theirs'.

One suggestion will be that the vehicles carrying money can be fitted with the likes of Scud Busters that America used against Iraq in the Middle East. These busters were activated by the sense of missiles in the air. So if our Cash-in-Transit vans have such sensors and blew the vehicle carrying the bombs, before the bombs blast the cash van, we will have no Heists.

But wait, our Law will come down heavily for killing the would-be criminals, who were innocently passing by on their way to kill mosquitos and green flies somewhere in the wilderness, with their bombs. Small wonder we frequently have bank notes flying all over the Freeways. It could well be perceived as a new invention of poverty alleviation. Because, ordinarily, one seldom picks up a bank note on the road, but following a cash-van can land a lucky citizen a bumper Lotto. If, of course one survives the blast.

Just to show how criminals undermine our law, recently in Boksburg, two cash in transit vans were blown to smithereens in broad-daylight, in a residential area. Men with heavy calibre rifles were seen waylaying these cars. Fortunately they never used them bringing in the question, what if they had to use them? How many innocent people could have been caught in the cross fire and injured or killed?

As if to answer these questions, on the 22 May 2018 page 1, the Star newspaper reported a cash-in-transit heist opposite Jabulani Police Station in Soweto. Unfortunately this time a woman was shot. This raises a question, is it fair for innocent people to be shot at while they themselves cannot defend themselves. Shouldn't the Constitution be amended to allow people to defend themselves against these heists and in the process assist the police? Can the injured claim compensation from the law enforcement department because we are warned on a daily basis never to take the law into our hands.

In that article, The Star highlights the important coincidence of the robbery being committed on the day that the suspects in the Boksburg heist appear in court. This just shows that criminals are having a field day and evidently do not fear the police.

We usually expect political parties to brief us on how they intend to deal with crime in their campaigns like 2019 national and provincial elections. Interestingly, South African Political Parties, were vigorously concerned when 52 Palestinians died and hundreds injured, in Israeli/Palestine skirmishes, (14 May 2018, The Guardian Newspaper). This was the time when Israel shot Palestinians during demonstrations against US opening an embassy in Jerusalem. That was right and commendable, we expect the same reaction from them in the Glebeland killings, Western Cape killings, KZN political killings as well as the killing of police officers. Otherwise we are only making ourselves the laughing stock of the world to be seeing a speck in somebody's' eye while there is a log in ours, (Matthew 7: 3).

The comments made by the police spokesperson in such incidents are very thought-provoking. In this one, Colonel Lungelo Dlamini says, "We don't know how many suspects they were…" then he goes on, "I don't think the guards would know the number of people who attacked them…"

I believe and with my little or no knowledge of crime investigation, the 'I don't know…' rhetoric is a big bonus to criminals especially because it comes from a senior investigating officer. This because should a member of the public wish to testify in an ensuing court case, she/he will first have to disprove what the investigating officer said, with authority, even before you dispute the version of the robbers regarding their number. Small wonder the public is despondent in assisting the resolution of such cases.

I believe hard-core-facts are what courts consider to convict a suspect. One will then have to stand in the witness box to state categorically that this was the number of robbers. This means that will be one's last testimony because the robbers will ensure you won't appear a second time.

The Three-Rivers Dry Clean Murders

Before the reader muses why I am so concerned with the Colonel's comments and the concept of hard-core-facts. I wish to deliberate on a case that unfolded in the Vaal Complex in 2006. It was dubbed 'the dry-clean murder case'. In here three ladies were allegedly strangled during the night shift at a dry clean depot in Vereeniging. The case was dismissed for lack of evidence by the Magistrate, B Ewart, who further commented that the investigation was amateurish, page 1 The Star newspaper, 25 April 2006.

The Sowetan Newspaper reporting on the same case as the Star, goes on and highlight an important principle observed by the courts in passing judgements, 'Hard-core-Facts'. This was said by the Magistrate when for some reasons, which were not disclosed in the two Newspapers, he had to address Ms Moeletsi, the aunt of one of the three deceased ladies; and he said "Patience was necessary for justice to be seen to be done. The court deals with hard-core-facts and do not work with pressure from outside", page 6 of Sowetan, 25 April 2006. The Magistrate continued to remark that the accused were arrested without substantial evidence against them. One factor he pointed out was that the post-mortem results did not support the contention that the slain women have been pushed into the washing machine and strangled by hand. Then he remarked, "It is quite clear there is little or no evidence against the accused".

One thing I have to point out and the Newspapers were also in collaboration, the crowd inside and outside the court was very vociferous in denouncing the court proceedings.

This prompts us to go back and peruse the events that led to this remark by the Magistrate. First the initial investigating officer, Inspector Sello Molapisi, was removed from the case, page 2 of The Star Newspaper, 6 March 2006. No reasons were provided in court for the public to know, at least the Newspaper did not mention them, if they were divulged. So the public was left to draw their own conclusions. Not that the court was compelled to disclose the reasons, but it could have at least quelled the negative perceptions regarding some verdicts by the public.

This was almost two months after the case started on 17 January 2006. The incident happened on the 3 January 2006 as the Star Newspaper reported.

In this edition of the newspaper, 17 January 2006, Inspector Molapisi is reported to have been bitter that the court denied his request to deny the accused bail.

On this date that the investigating officer was removed from the case, the Newspaper reports that the case was transferred to another court, were the alleged two co-accused, Samuel Mzizi and Jacob Dlamini were granted bail. The paper further states that the newly appointed prosecutor, Advocate Christo Roberts told the magistrate, W

Hewitt, the states' case was weak. The case in the new court was greeted with an interesting remark by the presiding magistrate, "This case has been allowed to unravel and I am dissatisfied with how the court proceedings, (in the initial court) have been managed".

The magistrate ordered that a new Prosecutor be appointed, this time by the National Prosecuting Authority in Pretoria, (page 2 The Star 6 March 2006). On page 2, of The Star 8 March 2006, it is reported, Advocate Nadira Narrandes on behalf of the State, said that "the director of Public Prosecutions, had ordered that an application to exhume the bodies of Jocelyn Lesito, Victoria Ndweni and Constance Moeletsi be made to magistrate, so that forensic investigations could be carried out. He continued, it has yet to be determined whether the blood found at the scene belonged to the three women or the accused. The State also said it needed to match the finger prints collected on the day the bodies were found". The Advocate Theuns Janse van Rensburg for the other four accused, Charl Corlyn, Ruan swanepoel, Jacques Smit and Isabel Corlyn succeeded in opposing the exhumation. In addition, the advocate for the two accused, Mzizi and Dlamini, Isabel Volschenk, pointed out that "The issue of finger prints was questioned and revealed only after two months".

On the final sitting of the case on 28 April 2006, the magistrate B Ewart this time, lamented the poor investigative work by the police, dismissed the case and the accused were set free.

From where I'm sitting as an ordinary citizen of a crime riddled South Africa, I wonder what would have been the concluding remarks by the magistrate had the order to go over the investigation again, to match the finger prints and the blood and exhumation of the bodies. So part of the unfortunate work by the police would have been compensated by the discrepancy identified by the Director of Public Prosecution, which the court denied.

At any rate that looked like a plausible verdict until one bumps on the Mail and Guardian report of 17 January 2006, when the case was first heard in court. In there, while the Star and Sowetan newspapers concentrated on the racial connotations of the case particularly where Sello Molapisi angrily remarked that "had the accused been black they would have been denied bail, but because this time around they are white, things are done differently." The Mail and Guardian went a step further and added the part where Molapisi actually pointed out that the, "Forensic experts had yet to finish their investigations at the murder scene as the only two in the country were attending other cases somewhere". The heading of this M&G article by Fran Blandy is also very interesting, if one considers this, "Employees said to have witnessed Laundry murder".

It looks like, based on the Mail and Guardian report, Inspector Sello Molapisi had a strong case against the accused, had it not been issue of the 'Hard-core-facts'. Furthermore it looks like the Director of Public Prosecutions had actually agreed with Inspector Molapisi regarding forensic investigation. Had this been acceded to, the outcome would have been anything but poor investigation.

Armed with the notion of hard-core-facts that the courts rely on, I wish to draw, again, the reader's attention to events in the Free State.

Hard-core-facts in the Ace Magashule garage issue:

Somewhere above I pointed out verdicts or no verdicts on a particular issue have a profound impact on what we as South African citizens perceive that incident, especially if it involves misbehaviour or crime. That's the reason I remembered what the magistrate said in 2006 when I read about how two Shell garages were disposed of in the Free State.

Recently it was reported that two garages that were leased from Shell by FDC, (Free State Development Corporation), now belong to

Ace Magashule's long lost daughter who goes by the surname Malembe, (https://www.News24.com/SouthAfrica/News/magashule-and-daughter-in-cash-for-jam-property-scandal).

The first garage was in Phuthaditjhaba in Qwa-Qwa. In 2014, according to the employees of the garage, Ace Magashule paid a visit to this Shell garage together with his entourage. Employees were of the opinion that their Premier was about to take over the running of this garage and were elated by this turn of events. The long and short of this story is that after denials by Magashule's spokesperson and his daughter that they intend to scupper ownership of the entity, it now officially belongs to Malembe and that's according to the newspaper report.

The sad thing is that all the 65 employees in this entity lost their jobs. It looks like the then Premier, Ace Magashule, whether or not he was involved in the transfer of ownership, is not familiar with deals of this nature. As the leading custodian of rights of the poorest of the poor, his role was of utmost importance, particularly if the said employees did not have a Union. Unions normally negotiate, that the new owners inherit the existing staff together with their benefits. This is understandable as the man had literally run away into neighbouring countries to avoid the harsh realities of apartheid when unions were started by the Ramaphosas, in the late seventies-early-eighties. However that is no excuse as he could have sought advice from the same Ramaphosa who, it is said, facilitated the re-union of father and daughter. I have to point out that Ace, as was customary in the Jacob Zuma administration, denied all knowledge or involvement in this saga.

One employee is quoted as saying, "Since I lost my job at the garage I have not found a new employment. It has been very difficult for me and my family." I said above that when such atrocities are vented out on the poor and defenceless people, God is irked.

I'm quoting this story as it reminds me of a similar incident by King David in the Bible. Not only did King David rob Uria of his one and only wife, despite him, having countless spouses, he continued to organise his death, (2 Samuel 11: 1ff). God sent Prophet Nathan to David. Nathan related his infirmities as though they were somebody else transgressions. Nathan proceeded to ask David what he would have done to the wicked king, and David answered with severe anger, 'that man must be killed'. Nathan answered, you are that man, (Samuel 12: 7).

The parable helped David to realise how terrible is his sin, because by his admission, the wicked king had to die. Psalm 51, is a revelation of how David felt after coming to terms with his wicked ways. David is recognised by God as a faithful servant because he normally acknowledged his follies and repented. This may serve as guide to self-introspection to those who swindled employees in Qwa-Qwa of their jobs. It was inhumane, callous especially from a so-called freedom fighter. I personally and obviously do not believe that people involved in this deal were once freedom fighters. No freedom fighter will commit such a treacherous act, only a sell-out will. Hence I say repent and accept Jesus as your Lord and Saviour that you may administer with righteousness.

The Second Garage Transaction in Bloemfontein

It is the transactions of the second Shell garage in Bloemfontein that has interesting revelations. "Like the deal in Qwa-Qwa, sources familiar with the FDC's bid to sell the Botshabelo property have claimed that "Magashule's shadow loomed large over the deal". In this instance a man Richard Kudhuga submitted a proposal to buy the FDC property on which the Shell garage was erected, for R5.5m via a family trust. Surprisingly, The FDC accepted a lower offer of R4m, from Botlokwa Holdings, a company owned by Malembe.

According to the news report, this puzzling state of affairs was questioned, first, by those in the FDC internal corridors. The response from the officials of the FDC was that "The deal should not be queried as it is driven by Magashule." However as usual, "Magashule and the FDC both denied that the Premier had meddled in either the FDC's Phuthaditjhaba or Botshabelo deals."

News 24, reports that the signed deed of sale between Malembe's company and the FDC states the property was sold for R2.9m, (Magashule and daughter in money-for-jam property scandal, 07:41 31/01/2018, https://m.news24.com/).

Although it was later claimed that documents were mixed up between the QwaQwa and Bloemfontein properties when the applicant Richard Kudhuga queried why it was sold for so less, the matter ended up in the Bloemfontein High Court to be dealt with, and for hard-core-facts to settle the matter once and for all. The applicant's request was for the review of FDC's bid process and to set aside its decision to sell the property to either Malembe or the MMAT Trust.

In dismissing this application the Acting High Court Judge by the name Sharon Chesiwe ruled that "It is an extremely serious matter for a court to intervene in decisions that were taken by the elected representative of an organ of state [and that] if [an] open court has to intervene at all, it should be done in extreme circumstances." The newspaper report goes on to say the Judge stated, "there were strategic considerations that gave [Malembe or her trust] advantage, despite their considerably less costly bid." The judge did not elaborate on what the hard-core-facts that support the 'extremely serious matter nor what the strategic considerations' were. The assertions stated above are what made the Acting Judge to settle the case. If the facts were provided later, I extend my apologies.

As I stated above, verdicts form the cornerstone of our moral behaviour. They guide us on how we can do what we want to do within the confines of the law. Because the Judge did not give us this guidance, the public is then left to speculate and ponder what is involved in all the phrases the Judge used to determine the verdict.

This verdict threw me a number of years gone-by when Nelson Mandela signed the adoption of our Constitution in Sharpeville, Vereeniging on 10 December 1996. I also recalled what we are normally warned against when attaching our signatures to a document, 'do not sign, until you read and understand the fine print.'

Sharpeville is a walking distance from Boipatong. I could not resist the urge to see Nelson Mandela face to face. I actually wanted to tough him and 'feel this 27 years in jail for the sake of a better life for all'. Because he was always busy crisscrossing the country and the world, this then, was my opportunity; for obvious reasons I couldn't get anywhere near him.

I remember at the entrance to the stadium we were issued with copies of the Constitution of our country. Most people were marvelling at the Bill of Rights which also drew my attention. I skimmed it quickly and was caught by the clause regarding 'equality before the law'. Satisfied, I closed it and rushed for my seat because Rolihlahla was about to speak. I read it in detail later in my leisure time the following week and I saw nothing that relates to 'exclusive rights' to anybody because all of us are equal before the law. Was I so spell-bound on Madiba that I probably missed something from his speech that had to do with some people having exclusive rights than others? Did our government take us for a ride?

What the Acting Judge did was to make the public aware that we have been given what we never ratified. What we approved is not what was on paper and some 'extremely serious and strategic considerations' were added after we had approved it. So when did this happen, if indeed there such clauses? We can say with certainty that it was definitely not with Nelson Mandela at the helm. It could also not have been during Thabo Mbeki tenure. The most likely period, based on rampant crime and corruption statistics as well as the dawn of the 'ANC as opposed to individual conscience', is in the past ten years. If we use the correct context, during the Zuma ANC and not the Mandela ANC.

It is thus fair and just to request the government to disclose the reasons that underscore the extremely serious nuance and the strategic considerations that the Judge referred to. That means we may have to overhaul the entire Constitution particularly with the deplorable economic, social and political situation we find ourselves in. Secondly, by an inference from the said Judge, they might have been given a stern warning never to reveal these 'strategic serious conditions' lest they start a revolution. In other words those conditions or rather hard-core-facts are not for public consumption.

I wish to state it on the outright that tax payers pay organs of the state, some of whom we elected, for reasons of transparency and accountability. It is precisely the reason why the applicant, Richard Kudhuga, took the matter to Court so that he understands, as we all want to, the requirements and processes in a bid procedure, precisely to stem corruption. On a lighter note, that's the reason we have a term 'tenderpreneur'; the art of acquiring tenders using shady tactics. These tactics, which other people cannot apply because they lack political connection. Secondly, if one goes through Nelson Mandela speech at the inauguration of the Constitutional Court, one finds the forewarning phrase, "attacks on human rights of the people are invariably couched in innocent language, Line 19"

The Acting Judge obviously knew nothing about an extra R9m that the Premier's daughter will pocket when the deal was concluded. However her ruling certainly helped the State to be R9m poorer, (https://www.News24.com/SouthAfrica/News/magashule-and-daughter-in-money-for-jam-property-scandal).

It certainly doesn't make sense to continue paying tax. It is outrageous.

According to the report, the deal in Bloemfontein, like the one in Qwa-Qwa, ended up with 60 employees losing their jobs.

In conclusion, when the Free State Province had been fiercely 'Shelled', it ended up with 125 families in dire poverty, one individual incredibly rich and as usual no one to account for this wretchedness. Some in these 125 family units, I believe, wish that she should have remained missing until Jesus comes. Because her reconnection with her father, the Free State Premier, has brought misery to those affected by rampant corruption under Magashules' watch.

It is also very interesting that the Estina Dairy saga has ended with on one found guilty. Something tells me this dairy had to do with peoples human and political rights of the Vrede residents. This because one of the tenets of Apartheid regime was to swindle blacks out of their means of livelihood, especially their livestock. If that be the case then the Constitutional Court should have invoked their oversight powers to stop the rot.

In the parable of the rich man and Lazarus, (Luke 16: 19-31 JCM), more than 2000 years ago, Jesus Christ told the world there will be the Shell garage and Estina Dairy fiasco in the Free State. Maybe the entire Free State and North West Provincial governments should have headed the warning. Just for the record, the North West Province under Supra Mahumapelo experienced untold service delivery protests and the residents pointed their fingers at this provincial government in particular the Health Department.

In this parable, Jesus uses some interesting words, verse 19 says, 'the rich man, in millions of cash', was clothed in purple and linen and fared sumptuously every day. Verses 20ff, continue, the beggar Lazarus, was full of sores and was laid at the gate, desiring to be fed with the crumbs that fell from the rich man's table. The dogs made feast of the sores dripping with blood and abscess from this man. God cut the man's misery short by sending an army of angels to take him away because He, The Almighty, had already prepared a place for him, on Abraham's bosom. It is said the tycoon also died at a later stage, but unlike the poor man, was buried. The Word of God says this man was in Hades, when he realised the poor man sitting with Abraham.

Interestingly, I have always been of the opinion that Hell will only start some centuries to come, when Jesus returns. No! This is not the case, Jesus in this periscope, says it starts the moment people close the coffin with soil in the grave. Meaning the 'great gulf fixed' referred to by Abraham in verse 26, is the grave. This is revelation by Jesus Christ that the burning in Hades starts in there and it goes on and never stops. This means, the grave is for those that are not saved. Those who have been washed in the blood of Jesus, the Messiah, pass on to Abraham's bosom. That is why we have these words in the "He is not in here, for He is risen," (Matthew 28: 6)

The rich man requested Abraham to send Lazarus to bring water, but it was not likely. Lastly the rich man requested Abraham to send angels to go warn his brothers on earth, lest they also end up where he is. The answer was, they have Prophets on earth, and they can listen to them.

Actually this text makes some fascinating revelations.

The gospel of salvation is a warning to those who want eternal life. If you do not want to listen, you only have yourself to blame. God who is righteous and sovereign, has done everything possible for us to avoid eternal death. He warns now, while there is still time. The choice is ours. "If you hear God's voice today, do not be stubborn, as your ancestors were when they rebelled against God, (Hebrew 3: 15 GNB)

Equality before the eyes of Society.

In this parable of the rich-man and the poor-man, (Luke 16: 19-31), Jesus negates vehemently that poverty is an indication of Gods punishment for sin and wealth is Gods favour for the selected few. This parable evoked nightmares for me when I read page 6 of City Press, 18 March 2018 that a child had drowned in a pit toilet with human faeces at a school. The school had recently built proper toilets and the old ones never demolished. Mind you, we are 25 years into democracy.

Now compare this incident with the Gupta child whose wedding was glorified with money meant for the poor would-be farmers in the Estina dairy project, in the Free State. We are told flowers only for this wedding, were worth hundreds of thousand rand. How do we face Jesus Christ to explain this rampant and chronically skewed distribution of wealth?

The disaster of South Africa and all countries that once experienced colonial oppression, is that those who ran away from the oppressors under the auspices of freedom fighters, came back to usurp economic responsibility from those who know better about the economy, the Union leaders. It is tragedy that will haunt us for decades to come that because people managed to run away from oppression, they are suddenly or miraculously experienced in running away from accountability. When this is questioned, the sceptre of 'regime change' mind-set is raised. Surprisingly, South Africa has shifted into Indian Monopoly capital and I have yet to hear of people running to neighbouring countries to fight this newly emerging scourge. Quite interesting!

It is a demeaning blight that South Africa, with so many minerals and industries, still has to make do with children drowning in the Juskei and Kwazulu Natal rivers when it rains. It is equally disturbing that those who were in charge, prior to Cyril Ramaphosa administration, denied involvement in decadence of the country's wealth.

That South Africa is a country riddled with corruption, is unquestionable. It is equally unquestionable that this corruption is a river that feeds in all fabrics of society because it had its source in Parliament. How this source is nipped in the bud is a task that is arduous even for our courts. The advent of Cyril Ramaphosa's administration is a beacon of hope for a better life. I understand he was the president of the Student Christian Movement in High School. This means he is a disciple of Jesus Christ the Savoir, so justice or justness will be a cornerstone of his management.

While discussing the tragedy of this little girl, it is worth noting that drug usage devours our country and in particular our youth. It is rumoured that the drugs originate from up North in Africa and they are specifically meant for our youth, our future government. It is not difficult to work out why this is directed at the cream of the society, the youth. It is so that foreigners can get this country on a platter, without even having to fight. This is what the Indian family of the Guptas has successfully achieved by their connection with the highest leaders in our country. And as usual, it does seem our courts will never be able to stem this line of corruption that will ultimately lead to the loss of our country.

With the level of lawlessness in the country, a question usually crops up whether our courts of law are still value for morality and sound ethical behaviour.

That is why I am writing this manuscript. Precisely because when God send Prophet Ezekiel to the stubborn nation He said, if you do not talk, because of the fear of being persecuted, their blood I will demand from your hands. But if you talk, you shall have saved your skin. The wicked will have reserved his/her place in Hell, like the rich man, (Ezekiel 3: 18-19). I hope somebody is shouting Amen!

8

"South Africa belongs to all who live in it"

One clause in the South African Constitution is that the country belongs to all who live in it. The spirit of this notion was to drive the message to the apartheid oppressors that black South Africans have a right to stay in it. That spirit has unfortunately been abused by foreigners who cross into the country and instead of shying from breaking the law actually lead the pack in the infringement.

Presently, eight police officers are in jail for the Death of a Mozambique man, Mido Marcia, while seven or eight South Africans who witnessed the shooting of Senzo Meyiwa are still roaming the streets. Surprisingly, Political Parties and the South African Human Rights Commission are usually quiet when foreigners assault police officers and the general public.

In the former case, the victim Mido Marcia was instructed by the two police officers to remove his car that was obstructing traffic. He objected and a scuffle ensued that lead to his death and the eight police officers involved were convicted and sentenced to 15 years each, on 11 November 2015, according to EWN report. What started as an offence carrying a minimum sentence of a R50.00 fine by the standards then, ended up with eight families facing a bleak future with their bread-winners locked up.

While South Africans are convicted the world over, in most instances for being used as drug mules, I have yet to hear of a foreigner assaulting a police officer there. I checked the internet, it happens only in South Africa and nowhere else in the world. This is because of our Constitution, it is a disaster for the South Africans, of the Apartheid era to be a playground for foreigners. If you do not believe, go highjack a building or obstruct traffic in New York, London or Botswana.

The reader should be aware that I am not disputing the verdict in the Macia case. I am merely suggesting that it should have been a stepping stone to the solution of similar cases. I sometimes wish it could have happened in the new dawn era of Cyril Ramaphosa and not the crime riddled era of Jacob Zuma. Maybe Meyiwa could be resting in peace knowing his killer or killers are serving sentences in jail.

One reason I have identified for this discrepancy, is that foreign countries will always raise concern when their citizens are killed in South Africa, even threatening to intervene on their citizens' behalf. This is in stark contrast with the laissez-faire attitude directed at 'Apartheid-era-black-people.' For South Africans, of the Apartheid era, they have to understand that they cannot take the law into their hands. The bulk of the murders in the Capetown, the Mother City, are South Africans of the Apartheid era.

The turf war for voters is behind this spate of lawlessness because any party that undertakes to kill armed robbers on the spot, will be counteracted by another party that will be soft on criminals under the assertion, 'criminals are human beings or the constitution of South Africa values life…' and all those meaningless and hollow statements. If you do not believe, let just one teacher kill a student and listen to the comments of the official of education castrate the teachers. This despite the teachers being killed on an incremental ratio in schools.

How I wish we could have 'a special institution' designed to protect and value the lives of all, by changing the Constitution. If you value the life of the killer, why not value the life of the victim. Passing messages of condolences is not the core function of members of the three arms of government.

As if this was not enough, on the 27 August 2019 in Pretoria CBD, a taxi driver was shot by a Nigerian national when he confronted him for selling drugs to school children. The ensuing fracas and demonstrations against this murder resulted in ten murders.

The Nigerian government was quick to comment on this even threatening to send an envoy to investigate these allegations. Nigeria stopped all the emotional outbursts on getting the raw facts that of the ten victims, two were foreign nationals, Nigerians and eight South Africans. There was surprisingly, no comment from the South African Human Rights Commission which is normally vociferous when foreign nationals are attacked.

President Cyril Ramaphosa attended the funeral of Robert Mugabe and was booed because of the riots in South Africa. The hauling only stopped when he apologised on behalf of the country. Again no reciprocal apology from the African countries for the killing of South Africans. Looks like South Africans are just statistics and valueless.

Police action or inaction:

We hear so many times about police doing nothing or coming in late to apprehend criminals when called. This is compounded in most instances by mistakes committed in apprehending or stopping the said criminals. In some cases, locking people/criminal when it was unnecessary, which is referred to as Police brutality. This then results in litigations where the State has to compensate the victims. Again, I developed a keen interest in how our Police perform their duties, based on my elementary knowledge of protecting the public from criminals.

Incidents in the past:

I recalled a number of incidents that called upon our police to act. I must concede I'm not sure of the date, and the newspaper they appeared in, but it should either be The Star or Rand Daily Mail. Those have always been my favourite newspapers. Some of these happened during the Apartheid era, (Seventies' or early eighties') and I believe some happened post-apartheid, but they all worked their way into our courts of Law.

These cases developed in me the call, particularly as a fervent Christian, to differentiate between criminal and good behaviour. As a result I am sometimes startled when I read about outcomes of court cases in the present time. I end up saying, 'I thought this will be the outcome based on what I have come to learn about crime', bearing in mind that verdicts and police activity or inactivity have a profound bearing on how we behave as citizens.

I tried to trace these cases on the internet but I was unable to locate them. If I had money I would have approached an advocate or a lawyer to help me.

Dogs mating.

There's a story of a man that let his dog roam the streets somewhere in Meyerton, near Vereeniging. It ended up in a neighbour's yard and the unwanted male dog mated with the new found partner. This resulted in a fierce fight where the owner of the roaming dog lost his life. The case ended up in court. The ruling was, if the man had kept his dog leashed, he would still be alive. He has ruined the other man's business seeing he was going to start a dog breeding business. From that day, I learned to keep my pets in my premises, up until this day.

A Benoni man relieving himself

The other is the case of the man who peed next to a tree in a block of flats, somewhere in Benoni. He had just knocked-off from work and was rushing for a train home. A lady residing in a block of flats on the upper level was standing next to a window that was facing the man down. She notified her husband that somebody down there is flashing to her. The man descended and blew the lights out-off the peeing pedestrian. The court passed the judgement that had the man observed public indecency by-laws, he would have speared himself the injuries. The aggressor was provoked beyond control and is thereby acquitted.

A child in crèche.

During either the Soweto uprisings in 1976 or the rent boycotts in 1984, the Police were chasing rioters and a rubber bullet was fired which hit a toddler in a Crèche. The murder case was dismissed in the court because "had there been no riots, the Police would never have been required to shoot and kill the child". The case was closed and the police acquitted.

These cases were by no means racially inspired, because then, as it is now, we were told the Judiciary was and still is independent.

A baby shot by a fleeing robber at the back of its mother.

Somewhere in Johannesburg, a police officer mistakenly shot a baby at the back of its mother while trying to apprehend a robber. The Newspaper reported that the thug will probably face an additional charge of murder since his misbehaviour caused the police officer to commit the crime. I did not pick this case in subsequent newspaper editions. Hence I am not certain of the court verdict.

The point I'm making is that the preceding incidents have one clear message to the public and that is 'If you misbehave, expect to face the full might of the Law'

A court sanctioned deviation from the norm:

While trying my best to locate these cases on the internet, and could not find them, I bumped into the case, "Minister of Safety and Security vs Mohofe (200/06)[2007]ZASCA 21; [2007] 4 All SA 697 (SCA);2007(4) SA 215 (SCA) (23 March 2007), (http://www.saflii .org/za/cases/ZASCA/2007/21", 27.03.2018). The reader should please note that I do not have the slightest idea what the string of numbers and alphabets behind Mohofe stand for. I suppose they have something to do with reference number of the case. My interest in this case is what happened, how it was resolved and most importantly, what does it mean to me as an ordinary citizen of crime verminous South African community. Furthermore, what as a citizen should I expect from the police and subsequently the courts of Law in dealing with crime.

This case, in a nutshell, unfolded on the 12 March 2001, near the crowded corner of Bree and Rissik Streets in Johannesburg. A police officer, inspector Gerson Nemengaya was patrolling the area. Three man he suspected to be robbers emerged from a shop fleeing. Two of them were armed with fire arms. According to him, the standard procedure he learnt from the Police College is for him to identify himself to the robbers. This he did by shouting to the fleeing robbers that he is a police officer and they should stop. They kept on running and one of the thugs identified as Mr Banyana Sibeko, turned and fired a shot at Mr Nemengaya, but missed him because he divide to the ground.

The robbers continued running and Mr Nemengaya fired a shot in the air as a warning. This is still a requirement for police officers in such situations. He then fired a shot which hit Mr Banyana Sibeko on the leg. Sibeko was arrested and taken back to the shop which he tried to rob. Upon arrival it was discovered that Mr Johannes Mohofe was lying in a pool of blood, dead.

Mr Mohofe's mother instituted claims against the appellant (the State) for loss of support for herself and minor children of Mohofe, due to the negligence of Mr Nyemengaya because he fired a shot that killed Mr Mohofe. At this stage I wish to quote the relevant document, "Although it was discovered Mohofe had actually been shot by Sibeko when he opened fire on Nyemengaya, the claim is based on the negligent and wrongful conduct of Nyemengaya in alerting Sibeko to the fact that he was a policeman, thus causing Sibeko to shoot into a crowd of innocent bystaders". The document states, "The respondent had originally alleged that her son had been shot by Nemengaya. The trial court found that this was not the case, and accepted that Mohofe had been struck and killed by the shot fired by Sibeko. This finding is not in issue on appeal".

In my little knowledge of the law, I thought the case should have been closed on the part of Nemengaya, and damages claim directed to Sibeko. Now my biggest concern is the allegation that Nemengaya is guilty of 'wrongful and negligent conduct in doing what he was taught to be the first requirement when approaching a criminal, 'Identify yourself as a police officer so as to effect an arrest'. Briefly, he was guilty of doing the right thing.

This allegation doubtless explains why when we as members of the public seek an urgent intervention on the part of the police they sometimes do not come or come late when the robbers had long ran away. It is because the police can easily be prosecuted for following the correct procedure.

A number of inferences can be made from this act which is actually correct but wrong for purposes of damages claim.

Firstly, if Nemengaya did not identify himself at the crime scene and the robbers continued to shoot at the innocent bystanders, he would still have been guilty of dereliction of duty; why did he not identify himself?

Secondly the criminals now know that Police officers have little power to use their guns to effect an arrest in a pedestrian infested area. I believe this is why there is so much crime around taxi ranks. Although criminals can be as violent as they like because they use stolen weapons and cannot be linked to the murder weapon unless it is found in his possession, it is not so with police officers.

Thirdly, although Nemengaya was shot at, he was, following the court verdict, not allowed to retaliate. This means had the criminal managed to shoot him, it would have been a bonus weapon on his side and more crime was to follow.

The State appealed this finding and was upheld with costs. But on my side as a citizen, I definitely do not blame the police for their laissez-faire approach to crime, they do not know when right is wrong, equally when wrong is right! There is a Pedi proverb, "ke khomo ya moshate, o a hapa oa e hama, ho a tshwana feela," that is whether you act or don't, it still results in the same outcome.

Fourthly, what if Mr Nemengaya tried to effect an arrest without identifying himself and the thug shot him. It is not far-fetched to imagine the criminal identifying this ignorance of standard procedure as the reason why he shot him; 'If I knew he was a police officer, I would not have fired a single shot, I actually would have submitted myself to arrest'. A host of witnesses around there would have testified to this statement, that he indeed did not identify himself. This could have been a mitigating factor for the robber. We sometimes wonder why people are arrested for serious offences and in no time are back on the streets continuing from where they left off. A Court of Law is not a child's play.

The dilemma is; when you observe a crime being committed, do you call the police or do you turn a blind eye? When you are alone you fear being pursued by the criminals if you report and when there are a number of people present, you assume somebody will take the responsibility to report and ultimately no one reports. A moral dilemma by all standards. It is not fair to the community but unfortunately one considers his/her safety before acting. The irony is that crime does not have a nose to smell, tomorrow might be the not-willing-to-be-involved-by-stander's turn.

Service delivery protests

I commented above about the inaction of police in acts of misbehaviour. This can be observed where demonstrations occur when people have service delivery demands to local government. Sometimes, like recently in my Township Boipatong, one observes police not taking **immediate** action against demonstrators damaging properties like robots, burning tyres in the middle of the road, R59 freeway between Vereeniging and Germiston, and throwing stones at passing vehicles. They normally delay action and only later start chasing looters when property has already been damaged. This has become a norm.

Recently, when Kaizer Chiefs supporters ran riot at Moses Mabida stadium and damaged property in full view of all who watched TV, this delayed action of the Police was also observed. Mr Irvin Khoza, chairman of the PSL, in his report to the minister commented, if the Police had acted fast enough, damage could have been minimal.

This raises the question again 'How violent should the Police be in a violent situation'? Secondly, how fast should they act? Thirdly, what mechanism do they have to use before property is damaged like in the recent Mooi River toll plaza riots where a number of trucks were torched. One recalls the violent riots due to fees must fall at Wits University.

I am continuously referring to properties in my discussion. However if one considers instances where loss of life was incurred and days thereafter police had not acted or could not act to apprehend those who caused loss of life, then one comes to terms with the full impact of what Jesus Christ means by justice. It happened in Marikana. Four days after the event started and four people having lost their lives, two security guards and two workers on their way to work, police had still not acted to apprehend those responsible; this is what Newspapers reported and was said and shown on TV.

Political Parties refer to these demonstrations as peaceful, regardless of the four, some reports say ten, non-striking members and security personnel having lost their lives. The word violence only reared its head when the striking members were killed. How I wish somebody could take us through a crash course on how peaceful a demonstration is, where people lose their lives.

I myself had been in wage demand demonstrations during my time in a Union that was initially called MAWU, (Metal and Allied Workers Union) in the eighties which later changed its name to NUMSA, (National Union of Metal Workers of South Africa). The last thing our shop stewards allowed us to carry in those demonstrations were any form of weapon, be it 'Traditional'. Nelson Mandela once denounced these and said, "Take those weapons, and throw them into the sea, they have no place in our democratic South Africa." He was referring to the use of traditional weapons in KZN. Incidentally, Zulu people are a peaceful nation. I do not for once believe they are comfortable with the endemic violence in their province.

I just want to go through the invocations of events that led to the loss of 34 striking miners, reports say this number exclude those that it is alleged, were killed by the demonstrators. Taking it from the scene where armed demonstrators are squaring it up with heavily armed police. In this 'peaceful demonstration', one can see police retreating slowly and demonstrators, in a hunkering posture approaching them. When a row of threatened people, police in this instance are acting in concurrence, backtracking, you sense a tacit pre-instruction, 'Don't shoot until you are instructed to do so'.

The scene as it unfolded, was a do or die. Either the demonstrators win by killing the police and somehow get their wage increase or the police run for their lives. The pertinent question is 'Who was supposed to tell the police when to shoot' in that nerve shattering scenario.

Before we come to this analysis, I wish to highlight a number of issues. As the four people, remember some reports say ten, mentioned above were taken to the mortuary, the President of the country then, Jacob Zuma, took a flight to Mozambique, on some government business I suppose.

It is also of paramount importance for readers to observe that the President of the country has a secondary title called the Commander-in-Chief.

Before we tackle this subject, it is worthwhile to go back to Polokwane where Jacob Zuma was elected President of the ANC. Which meant ultimately President of the country. After this victory, (I wish TV could replay it), he held a press conference. Reporters there, were concentrating on his prowess to give crucial decisions. They particularly asked this question a number of times in different formats, 'how are you going to cope?', because this position requires crucial acumen in decision making? In all instances, Jacob Zuma emphasised 'the ANC collective' as responsible for taking decisions. He even said, in the ANC, we work as a collective, nobody takes unilateral decisions. This sounded reasonable as the outgoing President, Thabo Mbeki, was accused of the very same attitude, taking unilateral decisions.

I do not know if those reporters were prophesying that at some stage in your tenure, you will be firing Ministers of Finance, alone in the middle of the night, without the very collective you are referring to.

Back to Marikana, as the miners approached the police, South Africans waited with bated breath for the decision of the collective. But the collective could not get into gear to conclude the discussion on the table because the one crucial person, the commander-in-chief, in the collective, adjourned the meeting to attend some business in Mozambique. Nowhere was the notion of a collective proofed to be a fluke than in the Marikana massacre. This is my asseion then, Jacob Zuma and Jacob Zuma alone, tasked and bound by the constitution, was the person who was supposed to give direction in the confrontation at Marikana. The Police Commissioner and Minister of Police do not have the powers to overrule the Constitution, the President has. Especially in instances where loss of life is imminent.

Presidents the world over have this exclusive discretion by virtue of their power as commanders-in-chief.

Let's cite an example, in the USA, when the Seals, an arm of the USA army, cornered Osama Bin Laden and realised the only way out was to kill him, they contacted Pentagon. Barrack Obama, as the then commander-in-chief and President of USA, appeared on TV the following morning and said **I**, not the collective, said they should kill him.

In our case, a man who was then identified as the director or shareholder of the said company, Lonmin, Cyril Ramaphosa, gave an advice, 'use a concomitant force'. For some reason, the police who by law need to take instructions from their line command, were able to deviate from the norm to be instructed by company official. The rest is history. Just then the meeting in Mozambique came to an abrupt end and our man, Jacob Zuma, took the first flight back home.

Political Parties, EFF in particular, made a meal of the ignorant voters. During the run up to 2019 National and Provincial elections, I wrote them two emails requesting them to come out and tell the voters how they are to going to deal with violent crime. This in view of the fact that they spread the diatribe that the violent Marikana wage strike was peaceful. They never responded, because there is no alternative to this except to contradict themselves. Again, I believe the Constitutional Court should have set the record straight. How peaceful is the death of citizens exercising their rights not to join a strike and go to work?

This cannot be justice according to what Jesus Christ described. When some people are killed, we turn a blind eye, when others suffer the same fate, we show concern. We are all made in the image of God hence all equal before the law. If the 34 peoples' life's mattered so did the other none striking miners as well as security personnel that were involved. The unfortunate part is that 'we shall kill for Zuma,' no matter what. A leopard never changes its spots.

Furthermore if compensation is to be paid to the families of the 34, so should the others be compensated and the perpetrators apprehended. Please do not even mention they are in the 34 dead because the case was never investigated. Which brings us to the concern I highlighted earlier, how quick should the police act, and how violent should they be in a violent situation. Had they arrested the murderers we would not have had the blight now called the Marikana massacre. Moreover what moral standing should the community adopt? Selective morality?

Unfortunately, from that day, criminals realised that the guns Police carry are useless, unless somebody somewhere phones and say shoot, by then the officer will be lying in a pool of blood on her/his way to the graveyard. Hence the festering crime and Police killings. Do we then wonder why criminals have escalated their methods to bombs on freeways and malls with scant regard to the safety of people they maim and kill? No political party will ever say the Police should shoot to kill the robbers, for obvious reasons of losing votes come Election Day. If Jacob Zuma had given the 'shoot instruction', he would not have had the opportunity to crawl on his knees in Marikana. This was his first visit just before the local government elections, in 2016, in a gesture of, 'It's not me, baba'.

The reader should realise I am discussing the Marikana confrontation as it appeared on the TV screen, not what happened in the hills as the police pursued these people away from the public glare. Maybe it is worth noting that in my entire career as a Union member, until my retirement, it was the first and I suppose the last to hear of a union official who addressed members from a Police Nyala, through its window for that matter.

The use of high calibre weapons we see in the robberies nowadays could have been curtailed had we denounced the demonstrators' violent behaviour in Marikana rather than using it as a political weapon to score votes.

Talking about the moral behaviour, around the time of the Marikana incident, the South African public was greeted by a man, in the Sunday Times Newspaper (https://www.timeslive.co.3a7news), wielding a knife and plunging it into a man identified as a fruit vendor from Mozambique. I was alarmed by the quick response from the government and the Human Rights commission in condemning this incident. The case was in court on 21 April 2015. Four days after the first killings in Marikana, there was still no response from the government nor HRC. The guy who killed was identified and the last time I heard about him was that he was to face a seventeen year jail term. What are we telling this guy and those that want to do this in future? 'Some are arrested and others escape with impunity' and Justice? Public reaction? Police do not come or come late when we call them. Moral fibre?

Do you really wonder why political killings are so rife, especially in KZN?

9

The mind of a rapist:

The Bible being the Word of God, is actually a manual for moral behaviour. It answers all those disturbing characteristics of human behaviour, one of which is rape, now rampant in South Africa.

To avoid harm and possible death, ladies are given various advises, ranging from submission to rape. The usual advice is not to resist or fight the man, observe some marks on him to be able to identify him at a later stage. In the chemistry of what happens in the body of a man, does this help the-would-be-rapist to divert his mind from this terrible affliction? Does it dissuade or urge him to carry on?

The following story will help men never to rape. Take note I use the word help not stop, because each one is an architect of his own destiny; more so if one has all the facts.

In the book of 2 Samuel 13, we find the story of Tammar being raped by Amnon. As the reader goes through this scripture, I would like you to pay particular attention to mood swings that play out in Amnon.

Amnon was deeply attracted to his sister, (it was customary in those days to love and marry a woman you are related to) Tammar. This attraction developed into love to the extent that he wanted to have sex with her. In the long run he achieved his mission by laying a snare for her, (Verses 1-11). In a normal love relationship, we men will recall the many Helicopters, Maseratis and Boeings we normally promise our loved ones, just to satisfy this lust. This happens even in a marriage set-up. It's exciting or should I say a way of showing the importance of ones' partner. By the time the man ejaculates, he has built all sorts of fantasy castles and when they are demanded after the action the response is usually: my love, did I really say all that?

This then, is what happened to Amnon when he raped Tammar.

Verse 15, starts with a chilling remark, "Then Amnon hated her exceedingly". The amount of love he had before the act had reversed into hatred. This is part of the sex act. Again we men will recall the speed at which we sometimes collect our under-wears after the act, because, and this serves as a warning to rapists, as soon as you finish the act, for a momentary 1-2 minutes, you want nothing to do with the woman. It is not hatred per se. This is the reason Amnon chased Tammar away when he said, "Arise and be gone!" I am talking from a man's experience, (and my brother, if it does not happen to you, then you are the luckiest man on this Universe, keep up the good work!).

The fact is, what women feel before the act, is what men feel after the act, the other side of the coin is, what men feel before the act is what women feel after the act. I suspect this is another reason, besides hygiene, why Jacob Zuma had to take a shower after 'having sex' with Khwezi. For the first time, I agree he did one correct thing is his entire life.

This is the stage where men are usually confronted with the inter-jection, (Sies ha o sa re tanki, oso tloha feela tjee s'ka kgoho? English, Shame on you, you don't even say thank you, you just walk away like a cockerel..?). When women say this, it's because this is where they expect to be cuddled, kissed and pampered as much as possible, but men for a few seconds or minutes do not feel that way. It's like you can have a momentary breathing space before going nearer your partner again. That's why the Bible calls it hatred.

However, men normally endure the little discomfort and continue kissing and hugging, because a few minutes thereafter you may find yourself on your knees again!!! And this time one may be armed with a valid reason because the time you collected the under-wear in a hurry, you were going to phone the helicopter guy to hurry up! And the process goes on and on and on!

Sex can only happen between lovers who are married and have time to run the entire practise characterised by the highs and lows of mutual feelings. This reciprocated compromise of feelings is crucial. It happened to Amnon, unfortunately in a rape scenario. The wickedness of rape is that rapists do not know they will be severely needed after the act. Again, I suspect this is the reason our Law does not recognize how a woman felt after the performance, because rapists took advantage.

Women can be beautiful and there are beautiful women on this planet. When men look at them, we feel that merely touching her will spoil all the beauty. Some are attractive, not entirely beautiful. However the Amnon incident reveal one fundamental truth, sex or rather orgasm, is the same, no matter the beauty or ugliness. The Amnon who spend days pleading with Tammar to the extent of going down on his knees until he succeeded, turned into a vicious animal a few seconds later.

Coitus is meant to fortify marriage. It is never a one way process to satisfy a man, because man and woman are both equal, before the righteous God.

In a rape scenario, this sensation of momentary distaste to a women can be disastrous. Particularly when the rapist recalls he is going to be reported to the Police. As the women holds him tight, for him to continue because she is enjoying, to the rapist it is interpreted as restraining him from fleeing. Secondly, the sexy look from the woman, appealing for more action, is equally interpreted as a means to identify him at a later stage. Add to this the developing hatred and you have a recipe for murder. Some say it is a way of concealing evidence, I fully agree, but it could well be this nasty feeling men experience after sex that exacerbates the situation.

Ever visited somebody in prison and asked him, 'But tell me, now that you got what you wanted, why did you kill her?' and he answers, 'Eish! mfwethu, ha ke tsebe ho etsahetse eng -my brother I do not know what happened'.

The point I'm making is that whether a woman submits to a rapist or not, the possibility of her death is still lurking. To avoid this, and a warning to rapists, next time you want to reach a climax, look for a partner not a victim.

I close this discussion by mentioning that sex is, save Salvation, the best thing that God invented. Hence I never miss the opportunity to commend and thank Him on how He outdid Himself by giving us sex. How I wish rapists could see it my way. At any rate; the justice Jesus Christ speaks about says; "Though shall not kill", (Exodus 20: 13).

10

Black-on-Black violence:

This was the buzz topic during the Apartheid era. During that time it was blamed, and correctly so, on whites who connived with blacks to kill other black people. We can cite as example the Boipatong massacre, Katlehong, Kwazulu Natal as well as Nancefield and Jeppe hostel mass murders. In the last mentioned area, it was by fighting between ANC and Inkatha Political organisations.

Surprisingly these murders reached their pinnacle after the release of Nelson Mandela. The perception then was that the Government of the day was fanning the spirit of despondency especially among the blacks so that transformation can be derailed. We may recall that Inkatha Freedom Party name was attached to the finished ballot paper because the party, for reasons best known to it, did not want to take part in the elections.

To cut a long story short, the situation was normalised and by the first election in 1994 peace was reigning in South Africa.

Unfortunately this phenomenon has again reared its head and it looks like we are again headed for pre 1994 era. This time it is not political parties on each other's throats but the selective manner in which this crime is handled, in some cases we see political parties responding to it by virtue of who is murdered.

May I mention on the outright that the topic does not include the Afri-Forum outbursts that there is mass murder of farmers. Not because there are no farmers being murdered, there are, but the genocidal manner on which it reported this incident did not match the facts on the table.

Blacks and Whites in Marikana.

Owing to my experience as a Unionist or a former Numsa member, until a few years before my retirement, I know for a fact that in every industry there are blacks and whites employed. I am also familiar with the fact that almost all incidents of dissatisfaction leading to the downing of tools are initiated by Black Unions because Blacks have always been on the receiving end of deprivation. I am also party to the notion that when Blacks go on strike, whites keep on presenting themselves for work, without any shred of intimidation.

It is not surprising that of the people murdered in the initial stages of the strike there by Amcu members, all victims were Black. In spite of whites doing the same thing done by the Black victims. The reason for this is not very far. Black life is very cheap and I mean Black South African life by this assertion. I have already touched on this topic above in the same incident. There I mentioned that when foreigners are killed in this country, their Governments stand up for them. That's not the case with our government. It has become a norm that a South African Black must die at least per day. I have also mentioned above how the EFF made a killing in terms of membership by disregarding the initial deaths committed by Amcu members and throwing upsurges regarding the 34 'dedicated cadres.'

As if that was not enough, in the Al Bar Shir controversy in Paliament after the altercation between Jacob Zuma and Musi Maimane leader of ANC and D.A. Julius Malema was the first to rise up to congratulate Jacob Zuma for not arresting the Sudanese President, this was on 07 April 2017. This in spite of the culprit being high on the list of world most wanted criminals by the International Criminal Court for five charges; Murder, extermination, forcible transfer, torture and rape, (https://www.icc- cpi.int>darfur>albashir). The reader should please note that Al Bashir is now standing trial in his home country where the charges do not include rape as in the ICC charge sheet. I have already discussed murder above, Sudanese are black people. Say this was done by Donald Trump and he, Julius Malema was called upon to react. I certainly know it would not be necessary to call for his response, it would have been spontaneous. Because in a political game, it is accepted for black people to be pawns for sacrifice by their black brothers whom we call freedom fighters.

I also mentioned the incident of Israeli and Palestine skirmish above, which took place on 14 May 2018. Again Julius Malema was the first to call upon Cyril Ramaphosa to recall the South African Ambassador in Israeli and expel the Israel ambassador in South Africa. A few months thereafter, 28 July 2018, 11 taxi drivers in a Quantum taxi, who were from a funeral of a victim of taxi violence in KZN, were mowed down by who, I don't know, however taxi violence, so far is between black people. I was woken up by the noise shattering silence from the EFF. Not surprising, a comment would have irked the potential voters.

The point I am making is that this selective manner of comment is sending a wrong message, such as it appears it is a good thing to kill blacks, as long as it's done by another black person. It only becomes an issue if somebody not black, kills a black. Please take note that by black I am referring to an Apartheid-era-black-South Africans, because they are the only ones who have no spokesperson. Because Al Bashir, a black person, is accused of annihilating other blacks, by a white monopoly capital court, we can live that, just so long as the murderer is not a white person. That's the position of our possible future president.

I just want to comment on the fifth charge levelled at Al Bashir, rape. Seeing that Julius Malema stood in support of Zuma on releasing Al Bashir instead of handing him in for arrest. Does the EFF leader have a soft heart for men accused of rape? He did the same when he coined the slogan, "We shall kill for Zuma." Furthermore, does this mean Malema's outburst about 'rape that must be defeated' is just a fluke? (https://ewn.co.za.>2019/06/17>malema. The man who captured him correctly is Mondli Gungubele, "Former deputy minister of Finance Mondli Gungubele has inferred that EFF leader Julius Malema's only consistent position is self-gratification," (News 24 correspondent, 16:44 19/07/2019). The other assumption is that he, Julius Malema, just shot from the hip, obviously without checking the facts.

"Only Africans will be killed if death penalty is reinstated." These are the words of another EFF leader and spokesperson Dr Mbuyiseni Ndlozi, (The Citizen.co.za). News24, reports on the same subject, "Official data reveal that blacks in townships are more likely to be murdered than whites in farms. In addition, News24 reports Dr. Ndlozi, said "The creation by the racist apartheid regime of townships was deliberate. The intention was to keep Africans and blacks far from 'normal life' and in social and economic 'hell holes'. The current spatial and socio economic patterns of townships bear the scars of our apartheid past. The taverns that mushroom daily, even near schools, are as a result of bars and shebeens that were constructed to ensure alcohol abuse was the major form of leisure for blacks."

These utterances by the Doctor are meant to persuade us that even though more blacks are on the receiving end of murder, we nevertheless need to be contend that they can continue dying so long as we do not kill the murderers. Secondly, I disagree with him that townships are a 'hell-hole' and in there people are far from 'normal life'. We would not be having so many churches mushrooming in hell-holes. What turns townships into 'hell-holes' and away from 'normal life' is lack of services. The voters have said that countless times.

Thirdly, the doctor does not explain how alcohol, consumed by millions of people the world over, suddenly become an inspiration in the consumer, and black men in this instance, to go and kill. If its inhumane to kill the murderers, so is it inhumane to kill innocent victims and worse still turn a blind eye under the cloak of the legacy of Apartheid.

Similarly, this is the argument that was put forth when punishment was abolished at schools. It was said no theory in the world has shown that punishment encourages students to study harder. Somebody must have forgotten to add that, in the same breadth, there's no theory to proof that lawlessness at schools encourages students to study harder. Whatever was possible has failed and schools have turned into war zones and murder hives with unemployment soaring.

Again, these emotional outbursts by the member of the EFF, amount to the rhetoric that black life is cheap and it can easily be swapped for a seat in Parliament. I want to reiterate my question, what is the EFF going to do, that has not been done already, to curb murder and rape, when it gets into power?

Put the other way, how should a Police officer apprehend a thug stabbing a victim in the congested alley of Small Street in Carlton Centre, Johannesburg in broad day light for that matter?

The tirade about apartheid certainly does not hold water because we have a black government in power and are twenty five years into democracy. At twenty five years you are no longer young. You have grown up and can start a family. So is our democracy, it can't forever stay young. The EFF looks set to take over from the ANC.

I certainly do not believe that the EFF has an answer to this pandemic.

Again, shouldn't the Constitutional Court intervene seeing that the right to life is being eroded with no reprieve in sight?

11

Conclusion

"Christianity has at its centre a Person, Jesus Christ. It amounts to much more than merely a moral system. This Person we accept as the revelation of the Father, The Son of God. It is from this and other associated fundamental dogmatic truths that much significant Christian moral teaching flows. Because Jesus has overcome the human limitations both in life, that is sin and death in His Resurrection. He has become Lord of ALL. He now offers a share in this life through the power of the Holy Spirit. He is a way to the new life, a new mode of existence. In ethical terms, we speak of Him as a formal, universal, concrete and personal norm of our Christian morality,"

(TEEC booklet 1 on Ethics 2011: p12.2-12.3).

Mandela and the Jesus mirror

I have drawn extensively from the Bible, primarily because when Nelson Mandela inspired the tenets of good governance and morality in South Africa, he drew them according to the 'being' of Jesus Christ.

On the outright I mention his likeness to Jesus regarding being humble, always ready to forgiveness, kindness, courage, and temerity as well as servant attitude to the people, by which he was known. It is a direct copy of who Jesus Christ is, even on His way to the Cross. Further more one can mention some of Mandela's quotes:

Jesus said, "If anyone wants to be the first, he shall be last of all and be servant to all" Mark 9: 35. Similarly, Mandela once said, "It is better to lead from behind and to put others in front, especially when you celebrate victory, when nice things happen. You take the front line when there is danger. Then people will appreciate your leadership."

Mandela speech characterised by the famous phrase, "It is in your hands" which he delivered in July 2007, is similar to Jesus', "The King-dom of God is in your hand", (Luke 17: 21; Mark 1: 15).

Nelson Mandela loved children and had intense compassion for the poor just like Jesus Christ did.

My sincere belief is that had Nelson Mandela just once mentioned that he drew his strength, wisdom and integrity from imitating Jesus Christ, we would not have had the satanic regime similar to the past administration of Jacob Zuma.

Admittedly, if he said it, then I never picked it up, and that's no fault of his. In that case I apologise with all my heart.

Not to be outdone is our President now Cyril Ramaphosa, Isaiah 6: 8, thuma mina. At least the Bible was written long before Bra Hugh Masekela was born.

As South Africans, we are stuck between a rock and a hard place. How do we remedy the situation?

Recommendations.

Firstly: We need to forgive those who wronged us: "Remember when you forgive, you heal, when you let go, you grow." (Anonymous)

In the Citizen Newspaper of 23 October 2017, page 1, it was reported, "How the Guptas stole SA Jobs". The report states how the Department of Home Affairs is now firmly under the control of the Guptas, where they issue residents' permit to foreigners who now occupy jobs that were meant for South Africans. Carrying a heavy load of hatred because of people whose mission is solely to destroy the country will not yield any fruit. In addition, and this is worth noting, we should remember that Hinduism and Islam want nothing to do with Jesus Christ and will stop at nothing to win His territory and set His subjects against one another.

"Go to the Lord, and you will live" (Amos 5: 6).

Page 2, of Business in Mail and Guardian, 27 October- 2 November 2017, titled "Tax evaders: Blame the Guptas". The courts are used by the National Assembly to ensure tax collection, but those same courts are mummified when the treasury leaks. Never-the-less, we need to continue paying tax to feed them.

Secondly: Abolish the office of the Public Protector.
In his inaugural speech, in 1995, at the inception of the office of the Public Protector, Nelson Mandela introduced the Government's National Development Plan 2030. He touched on the government's political will to fight corruption and providing sufficient funds to institutions

that combat this scourge. He also mentioned "the independence of the anti-corruption authorities from political interference and the consistency with which the law is applied". These goals were achieved from our first Public Protector, Selby Baqwa up to Advocate Thuli Madonsela. The same cannot be said of Advocate Busisiwe Mkhwebane. She is actually a stepping stone to corruption and crime.

The office of the Public Protector is intensely abused by the Cabinet and thus a hindrance to the police to fight crime and corruption. This office has proved the disaster of an institution that is both a player and a referee. Her dismal performance was shown in her first and unnecessary case where she strived to change the mandate of the Reserve Bank. Like in a relay race, she had just assumed duties from Thuli Madonsela and the whole country was anxiously waiting to see the outcome. And boom! There she came up with something nobody expected. That case proved beyond doubt her gross incompetence and she should have been fired on the spot. Without pay.

I then suggest to dissolve the office of the Public Protector, immediately and incorporate it into the SAPD. This will save the country a lot of money while duties are not duplicated. Ever wondered why potholes are like spring flowers all over the country, it's because the local government points to the provincial government, which in turn points to the national governments and the wheel turns around in reverse. The office is easily manipulated by politicians, especially if the incumbent is as weak as the present candidate.

Thirdly: Replace the judges of the Constitutional Court:
I have discussed the debate in the Constitutional Court, between the defence Advocates and the Judges. This Court identified the separation of powers of the three arms of governance as preventing it from doing anything against Jacob Zuma. I completely disagree with the Judges on

this card. Firstly because they were called upon to adjudicate on **the ANC that refused to expel Jacob Zuma**, not on who should expel Jacob Zuma. Secondly, based on what Nelson Mandela said in his speech at the inception of this Court, it is clear that they were given enormous powers to act beyond the scope limited by the separation of powers should an anomaly arise, as in this case. Consider this, "What this case is about, is that you have the head of state taking public funds for personal use, the ANC in Parliament is in the majority and can decide to keep Zuma,"(Advocate Tembeka Ngcukaitobi for EFF), this appears in the reference link. Add to this the hot rumour that Zuma ran the country from Saxonwold, the Gupta residence.

If we replace the board of directors of Standard Bank, with our Cabinet, you end up with two institutions that both were confronted with a damaging rumour. One is disciplined by its special institution and the other is left to be a law unto itself. I cannot explain it any further. The irony of all this is that it is not difficult to work out why the ANC members did not want to vote against Zuma, because if the outcome did not put him out, those who voted against him would have lost their life time benefits because he would have demoted them in the middle of the night.

In the past, petrol was rationed in South Africa during certain hours, because of the government laws. Mind you, we did not even have a Constitutional Court then. Judges used to go a step further, on their own and authorise garages to open for people to reach their destinations, much against the proclaimed laws of the country or the separation of powers. This is what law-abiding citizens expected in the Nkandla issue. We should all remember that Jacob Zuma was accused of a crime, not a work related misconduct like absence without leave or drinking at workplace.

Crime is dealt with in the Criminal Court not in Parliament.

This prompts us, again and again, to dig deeper into what was on Mandela's mind when deciding on the formation of the Constitutional Court. It is clear that its powers were discussed and agreed on and it is also clear that Justices in that discussion were quite aware that Mandela proposal was not practical, if the notion of the separation of powers is anything to go by. Because by the arrangement of the separation of powers it would not be possible for a court or judiciary to override the powers of the other two arms of governance. The fact that they agreed for this Court to come into existence, knowing fully well its powers cannot exceed those of the other two arms of government, is tantamount to fraud. The Constitutional Court has failed South Africa in that case and it failed us dismally. I definitely recommend the replacement of those judges.

Its purpose now is to be a rubber stamp (Line 43-44) decisions of the ANC majority and to throw the whole maintenance of sound judiciary into disarray. The Honourable Justices need to be replaced by Cyril Ramaphosa. If that is not possible then we need a referendum by the South African public on its continued existence.

If Jacob Zuma was tried by a Criminal Court for stealing, he would be telling people now, 'please do not do crime, it does not pay'. Instead he is inciting everybody who is conveniently ignorant, that he does not know what wrong he has committed, ' Nelson Mandela on 'innocent language,' lines 17-19). He would be knowing exactly what his crime is, thanks to the Constitutional Court. The Constitutional Court by its own admission that he committed a crime, should have referred the Zuma case to the Criminal Court not the Cabinet. The Cabinet is not a Court, let alone for criminals.

To make two simple illustrations.

The Standard Bank and Afriforum:

"Yet experience everywhere teaches that in addition to all this, the criminal justice system, special institutions are required to ensure the continuity of right and justice."(Line 29-30) This by no shred of doubt places the Constitutional Court in the centre of organizations meant to combat the flouting of the Constitution.

Firstly, if we scrutinise some of the special institutions in the world, which Mandela refers to in his speech we may be very close to grasping what he had in mind by special institutions. Secondly we need to take note that because the broad South African society did not know about these special institutions, Mandela speech is crafted in such a way that it divulges the core functions of this institution, that is, what South Africans should expect from this new and special institution.

This can be confirmed by asking relevant questions; such as, did the Constitutional Court act according to the stipulations of the constitution when it referred the Jacob Zuma case back to Parliament for trial? The answer is an unequivocal yes, they were 100% right because that's what the Constitution dictates. The second relevant question is, did that help South Africa curb crime, corruption and State Capture? No! Add to this the many demonstrations that called for Zuma to step down. If the Standard and Absa Banks' special institutions could act on the strength of a rumour, our parallel special institution in the name of the Constitutional Court was duty bound to act on the strength of the public demonstration that were reported all over the world by the media. The demonstrations were the result of the concern that corruption emanates from the highest office in the land and that office was that of Jacob Zuma as president.

The Constitutional Court as it stands now, the only thing special about it is that people can by-pass the Appeal Court in Bloemfontein and seek assistance from it. In addition, by Mandela standards, the last thing he had in mind was for this special institution to be an advisory body on matters that result in insidious corrosion of individual human rights, (Line 18). This Court was designed to be the final arbiter in matters affecting violation of constitutional rights. That means it has to give verdicts not lectures on ethical behaviour.

If this is not what Nelson Mandela had in mind about this Court, then by all means South Africa does not need this toothless and clawless bull terrier. The judges must be replaced every five years. From where I am sitting, I strongly believe the Guptas pinpointed this loophole, before destroying our economy.

Likewise when the rumour surfaced that the president, in this case former President Jacob Zuma, was involved in crime, we expected the Court to scrutinise the Constitution to find out what is in there that gives the President a lee way to commit crime which ultimately devolved in rampant corruption, and make the necessary alterations. The fact that Jacob Zuma had to go borrow money from VBS bank, is a clear indication that, as stated in the then Public Protector's report, Advocate Thuli Madonsela, he had committed a crime. The Constitutional Court, as per guidelines of their discussions with Nelson Mandela, should have redirected the case to the Criminal Court. This then brings us to the same question, does South Africa still need this Court?

His speech gives the South African public an idea of what he had in mind by recommending a special institution to guard against insidious corrosion, of peoples' rights. The Guptas made off with billions of our money to Dubai and the country is left to fend off countless service delivery protests because of that. Do we still need this court?

The ripple effect of crime and corruption in the Zuma administration, was the establishment of the following commissions, Tax by Justice Nugent, Justice Lex Mpati for PIC, Justice Mokhoro on Lawrence Mrwebi and Nomcgobo Jiba fitness to hold office, State Capture by

Deputy Chief Justice Raymond Zondo, which among others, revealed wrong doing by Bosasa. In the last mentioned commission of inquiry, Andries van Tonder the CFO of Bosasa mentioned that the owner, Gavin Watson's name does not appear on the Special Investigative Unit report because he signed no documents, just like Zuma in Parliament.

This is something that could have been avoided if the Constitutional Court had executed its mandate as agreed with Nelson Mandela. The Zondo commission of Inquiry into State Capture reveal how the board of directors in all State Owned Entities helped loot the finances taking the cue from the President of the country. Does this court have any capacity to stem crime now, seeing that it missed the boat in this instance of a corrupt president? Does South Africa still see any know-how for this court to stem crime and corruption?

Our State Owned Entities are in a dire situation because all the officials were politically connected to the president in the name of Jacob Zuma.

Just to show that the Cabinet under Zuma was a law unto itself, in the Al Bashir case, not only did the Cabinet defy the High Court in Pretoria, but Zuma opened the debate in Parliament and told the opposition party, leader Musi Maimane of the Democratic Alliance, that the law does not allow him to hand a visiting head of State in for arrest. In the interest of separation of powers, I thought he would respect the court order. The Constitutional Court should have pointed to the unconstitutionality of this stance by Jacob Zuma and the Cabinet. Incidentally, is it not an offence to defy a court order? If that be the case, then we need to be made aware that court orders are no longer worth the papers they are written on.

Jacob Zuma was defiant to a court order knowing fully well that he is under the protection of an ANC majority and he also knew that if he had to stand trial for this, it will be in the Constitutional Court not the

Criminal Court. Does South Africa still see value in this Court? Personally I don't. These judges must be replaced. Nelson Mandela had good intentions when he formulated this Court, unfortunately the respect the South African public has for the office of the President has been demeaned by Jacob Zuma in ceding his powers to the Guptas. This is testimony from the Zondo Commission of Inquiry.

The Constitutional Court must be revamped, so that through the Criminal Courts, South Africa can deal effectively with crime and corruption. Mcebisi Jonas and Themba Maseko in their testimonies in the Zondo commission of inquiry, gave a clear picture of how the Guptas fermented corruption through their connection to Jacob Zuma. Their tentacles through this connection ran deep into the SOE's. The SAA, was under Dudu Myeni and it made terrible losses that were falsely assigned to hidden-hand-of-the-white-monopoly-capital. The Zondo Commission of inquiry reveal how the then President Jacob Zuma, was neck deep in fermenting corruption at SAA. The Constitutional Court judges must be replaced.

The special institutions that Nelson Mandela refers to in his speech, have the special powers to intervene in all instances of abnormality, and most importantly, they did not have to be invited by those whose rights were violated. Hansard was spot on when he said, "Persistent contravention of human rights is a recipe for violent conflicts and war,": Debate on Human rights Day: From Oppression to Human rights-Centred National Democratic Society, 15 March 2010 in the joint sitting NA +NCOP, (https://pmg.org.za>hansard.)

Violent conflict and war is what we see on the streets of this country because of men and women in the Constitutional Court who could not give a verdict on, Jacob Zuma.

The fact that the Zondo Commission of Inquiry wants to recommend a Commission of Inquiry into why ANC members of Parliament failed to exercise their oversight responsibility regarding Zuma is really a waste of time and money because we already know the answer. The answer is that the ANC majority did not want to, and no one including the Constitutional Court could force them to do it. The opposition parties in their submission to this Court stated exactly that, the ANC does not want to discipline Jacob Zuma.

The way I see it, Judges of the Constitutional Court, should be the ones invited to this Commission to give reasons why they failed to rule on Jacob Zuma. That will mean The Commission will have to be under a new steward, not Deputy Chief Justice Raymond Zondo. After finishing his work as chairman he can lead the pack by taking the witness stand.

That is why I strongly believe and recommend that for the present government of Cyril Ramaphosa to deal with crime and corruption, the Constitutional Court cum Advisory Council must go to the waste bin. It cannot be the Highest Court with a Chief Justice at the helm and fail to give a verdict.

While trying to piece together the jig-saw-puzzle, particularly on whether these special institutions, mentioned by Nelson Mandela, have investigative powers; Chief Justice Mogoeng Mogoeng came to our rescue. In his speech on the 18 July 2019, delivering a lecture or sermon on Sixty seven minutes dedicated to Mandela at the Hope Restoration Church in Kempton Park he said:

1. "…will not be able to defeat corruption unless the narrative that it is a black thing is debunked…we have channelled ourselves into believing that corruption can only be in the public sector," https;//m.news24.com>News>corr…"

2. Somewhere again he says "…If they fund you to the point that you succeed and win and become a government, are you not captured in advance?" His speech on 17 July 2019, "Chief Justice highlights 5 key challenges for SA."

3   "… the perception that South Africa's problems would disappear once we have dealt with the Guptas situation because then we have dealt with corruption…will be a disservice to this nation, it is a fallacy… who else is benefiting from the coal issue at Eskom? Have we ever bothered to find out how much other people are getting."

In the first one, the Chief Justice states clearly that he has done an in depth investigation of the source of corruption in South Africa and has discovered that various nationalities, black, brown, white or yellow are involved in corruption. However it is only blacks that are being incarcerated or criticised. This stance by the Chief Justice clearly shows the Court has investigative powers and he has indeed done his homework. Now the question is who needs to arrest those other nationalities that are being ignored while blacks are arrested? If they are not arrested who needs to tell the police to do their jobs properly? The line functionary up to cabinet minister up to the President. If then beyond the President the street runs dead? The Constitutional Court should take over.

Secondly, are we ever going to end crime and corruption if we are in the business of balancing nationalities in our prisons? Thirdly, this statement is actually a political party manifesto, that when I get into government, I will make sure that not only blacks are identified as criminals but other nations as well. I therefore think that the Chief justice is in a wrong vocation. It may do him well to join a party like EFF because it harbours same convictions. I have already cited Dr Mbuyiseni Ndlozi and Julius Malema above. This, despite the fact that, there is a Black, not an Apartheid or white government in place.

Point number two of the Chief Justice, is a clear reference to President Cyril Ramaphosa, who is accused in court presently, by the Public Protector Busisiwe Mkhwebane, of receiving a blood donation from one, Gavin Watson, of Bosasa, for his presidential campaign CR 17. The first disaster of this statement is that, should Ramaphosa be found guilty by the lower court, he stands no chance of succeeding if he appeals the Constitutional Court, seeing that the verdict has already been pronounced, in a prayer meeting. Moreover is this statement by the most Senior Judge not a hidden instruction to the Lower Court Judges on what the outcome should be in this particular case? The Chief Justice is clearly biased against Cyril Ramaphosa, the President.

Secondly, seeing the Chief Justice is so generous in dishing out judgements, on every convenient platform, should South Africans still have confidence in the uppermost court in the country? Is it not time to renew this Court?

It is in the third comment by the Chief Justice, that I definitely recommend South Africans renew the Constitutional Court. When masses of South Africans through the Opposition Parties approached this Court in the Zuma criminal matter mentioned above, they did not **think**, as he states, they **knew** they will harness their billions before the Guptas ran away. The advice the court gave that the case be returned to Parliament, actually favoured the ANC and the Guptas. Seeing that the cabinet is not a criminal court, was there no possibility that if Zuma was voted out, he would appealed the CCMA or the Criminal Court?

The advice therefore puts the Constitutional Court squarely in the alliance camp, seeing that the ANC regarded the move by the opposition to remove Zuma as 'the demand of the enemy.'

If the Court is not abolished, is it not the right time to let the South African public have the right to vote for the candidate of Chief Justice, seeing that that position together with that of ministers in cabinet are the domain of one person, the President. If we were afforded that possibility, may be some would have voted Dikgang Moseneke as Chief Justice. There was a definite and muffled outcry on why Jacob Zuma overlooked him.

The question that the Chief Justice raises as to who else is benefiting from the Eskom coal fraud, is his realm to deal with. It again confirms the investigative mandate of this special institution. He did make an investigation but not for the benefit of the country. We get an impression that the perception that it is not only Jacob Zuma who is corrupt, but many others as well, actually influenced the advice from the Court. You people are dragging Zuma in here while you leave others outside, bring them all here if justice is to be done.

Poignantly, it is precisely because of that advice that raw sewerage is running, past our houses, into the Vaal River, damaging our ecosystem. Certainly because of that advice by the Constitutional Court to Parliament, that there are countless service demand protests, throughout the country. It is because of that advice that rogue units are a necessity even now. Pravin Gordhan must revive them.

I certainly believe that if Nelson Mandela were to come assess the country now, he would definitely be ashamed to have recommended the Constitutional Court and the Public Protector, for South Africa.

The Standard of the Law degree in South Africa

In The Star Newspaper, 3 June 2019, it was reported on the front page that the LLB degree offered at all South African Universities should be revamped.

On the same day, 3 June 2019, on page three, The Citizen Newspaper also published an intriguing report of five High Court Judges in Kwazulu Natal who sanctioned graft. Judges are our last line of defence in fighting crime and corruption. If that defence is leaking, we may end up with the answer why South Africa is a den for drugs and no known drug lord is behind bars, a hive of daily murders and the

Police being powerless to shoot criminals while they themselves can be shot at and killed.

In my mind what the two Newspapers report highlight, is not the quality of the text books, journals and manuals that are used in the Universities for the Law degree. It is the integrity, the ethical principles and behavioural dogma that goes with this office that does not change. Simply said, a criminal enrols for the Law degree proceeds right through to be an advocate and ultimately a Judge and she/he has not changed at heart. In Theological Language it is called in Sesotho, 'Moruti wa tsotsi,'a criminal pastor, and in Law, moahlodi-wa-sekweta, a delinquent judge.

It is clear that South Africa is losing the fight against crime and corruption. One of our weakest links in this fight rests with our courts that are fed half-baked information emanating from influenced prosecutorial decisions. We need the support of our Judges in a campaign against corruption and crime as much as they need ours. They also rely on tax payers' money for their livelihood.

While we're on the subject, the motivation to take up arms through Mkhonto we Sizwe, by Mandela and other comrades, was instigated precisely by the courts which were powerless to act without fear or favour. This despite the usual assertion that the judiciary is independent. Something which Dr Percy Yutar, in front of Nelson Mandela conceded was an oddity. This he said when he was invited by an ever-forgiving Nelson Mandela at a dinner party in 1995, (https://en. wikipedia.org>wiki>Percy_Yutar).

It seems very likely that Mandela pondered an organisation that will work, in the legal framework, to intervene in the event of violation of human rights. He did not want to go back to revive Umkhonto we Sizwe in a constitutional democracy. He then crafted Umkhonto we Sizwe however in a legal and constitutional frame work and called it a

Constitutional Court. We all recall that MK did not ask permission to take up arms, it acted spontaneously. The Constitutional Court was crafted in the same spirit. Nelson Mandela must be turning in his grave.

South Africans should unite to vote this Court out.

"Let us not grow weary while doing well, for in due season we shall reap if we do not lose heart". (Galatians 6: 9).

"For God will bring every work into judgement. Including every secret thing, whether good or evil," Ecclesiates12: 14.

Another recommendation is that it should be a criminal offence for the President, Premier and Mayor to give oral instructions only, on matters that enormously impact on peoples' rights. Written instructions will force them to demand written response from their subordinates. Then the courts can deal with written evidence and not be confronted with statements like; '…I do not know who said that and I did not even know such a thing was happening in my department.'

A clause should be included in the constitution where members of the public have a right to vote a sitting President out if the cabinet does not want to, like in the case of Jacob Zuma. Then they cannot hide behind the threat of expulsion and intimidation if they act correctly.

Ramaphosa to be President up to 2024 and beyond.

Lastly, at the time that this book was written, there were suspicions doing rounds that Cyril M. Ramaphosa received a R500000 donation from Gavin Watson of Bosasa for his ANC Presidential campaign. What looked like an innocent act of compassion, turned out to be a pre-determined time-bomb for hope to law-abiding South Africans. It reminded me of a text in the Bible, "Judas is it with a kiss that you betray the Son of Man," (Luke 22: 48).

A motion of no-confidence for Ramaphosa's removal may be tabled in Parliament, if this is true. I want to appeal to the South Africans to stand up and demand a re-run of the elections if this happens. Because as things stand now, we are faced with a situation where Estina dairy fiasco will turn out to be kinder-garden picnic. Secondly, we are headed for Local Government Elections. That will be the opportunity to do away with the ANC, starting from the bottom upwards in 2024. Nelson Rolihlahla Mandela will definitely have to rest in peace, we tried our best to salvage his legacy.

A Sea of Shells

Ostensibly, it is the level of determination and dedication shown by our Public Protector Busisiwe Mkhwebane, in pursuing graft on Ramaphosa, that left me gaping with amazement. If we do a little arithmetic, we can actually assign a monetary value to what we up to now called 'black life is cheap'. She dilly-dallied until the Guptas made off with our billions. They missed a trillion rand record by a whisker. However it was not so in going after the R500000 that tainted the President.

R500000 divided by R250000000, lost in Estina is 0.002 of a rand, far less than one cent. So what we initially called 'cheap' can now be valued at 0.002 of a rand. Unfortunately the half a million does not belong to the service delivery kitty, or the South African population, it belongs to Gavin Watson, dead or alive. So we are actually valued at zero for now, at least. Now if we divide half a million by forty to sixty billion rand, that should have been recovered from the Guptas, for service delivery, we end up with 0.0000125 of a rand. But wait, you may have to add a few more zeros before the 125 figure, if you add the losses our grandmothers experienced in VBS bank loot. Losses in VBS were, allegedly orchestrated by those who are now shouting the loudest for the recovery of the half a million rand, because, this half a million is worth not only a presidential seat, it is intended to deride him who has been denouncing corruption. Nowadays in South Africa, a seat in Parliament is acquired by denouncing ethical behaviour. That's why none of the forty to fifty parties contesting elections is committal to tackling crime especially of murder and I can assure you, none will.

What do I mean by this? The Estina Dairy fiasco can serve as a good example. A whistle blower and potential lead witness, Phillemon Ngwenya, (Suspiciously murdered), is now six feet under ground and I doubt if there will be anybody serving a jail term for his death, watch this space. Our Public Protector has closed the case because, as reported on a regular basis on Television, "It does not implicate the then Free State Premier, Ace Magashule." Meaning if Magashule was involved in that corruption, it would have been investigated further. This despite Daily Maverick reporting "Dubai: the Guptas' city of shells, 25 June 2019, News24. This report states that, from the #GuptaLeaks emails, "It is clearly shown that the Gupta brothers and their close associates have amassed a considerable collection of companies in the United Arab Emirates."

Below this paragraph, is a heading," Find all you need to know about #GuptaLeaks here." Details of how money left South African State Owned Entities to Dubai with the assistance of our highly educated CEO's of our SOE's, is revealed. These emails, out of the Gupta negotiations for their loot are what Busisiwe Mkhwebane found waiting for her when she took over from Advocate Thuli Madonsela. The fact that she closed the case simply because Ace Magashule is not mentioned is a clear indication of her hiding a bombshell. Fortunately, the court has rubbished her report and the investigation needs to be resumed, unfortunately and most unfortunately, by the NPA. Why? Ephraim Dhlamini in the Zondo commission, lists names, three in number of suspicious murders. He even showed NPA graft on video committed in the dairy farm, but nothing came of this. In his testimony, he implicates Msebenzi Zwane and Ace Magashule of being involved in siphoning money to the Guptas,(Google: Estina Dairy Farm: Witness lifts lid on explosive murder claims, implicating Mosebenzi Zwane).

The report states how Dubai is a sea of shell companies abandoned by the Guptas as they moved money from one to the other to conceal their laundering antics. We expected the Public Protector to be hard at work in Dubai trying to piece together how we were swindled.

My gut-feeling tells me somewhere in those emails, a discussion was held on how all those orchestrating the scam, the entire criminal justice system, would by-pass prosecution for initiating corruption in SOEs.' It can also be a reasonable suspicion that even if prosecuted they will not be found guilty. Interestingly, it is now over fourteen months that South Africa has been waiting for these emails to be played so that the public can judge for itself. Just like the Spy tapes in the arms deal saga that were stashed away, we are still waiting for the emails to read for ourselves. I believe just like South Africa heard from Jacob Zuma, the accused, that the tapes have nothing that incriminates him, we are probably going to get from him, again, that those emails have nothing to do with him.

Back to the black life is cheap, alternatively, we need to re-run the National and Provincial elections so that we can improve this value, if Ramaphosa is removed. We voted for ANC because of Cyril Ramaphosa, definitely not because of Ace Magashule.

I have always wondered why God made sure Jezebel in the Bible, hasn't got a grave. While Moses hasn't got one, at least we know where he is, because of Jesus Christ transfiguration, Mark 9: 4. But not Jezebel.

Secondly, our Public Protector is now after Minister of Public Enterprise for appointing rogue units to investigate graft on our Ministers. As far as I am concerned, we should have had more rogue units up to this day. What Pravin Gordhan did was supposed to have been done by the then president. He couldn't, because he was leading corruption, as stated by witnesses in the Zondo Commission of Inquiry.

The Stump: Isaiah 11:1

I wish to end my discussion by quoting Phllip J Wogaman, "This volume is explicitly Christian in its fundamental value assumptions, which means that in some way, it presupposes a Christian definition of the subject of moral commitment. There is a sense in which ethics is ultimately religious in nature. A non-religious 'secular' ethics is capable of dealing with the form of moral commitment and judgement, establishing regulative norms and criteria. But it remains uncommitted to any ultimate reference for valuation. Without such a context, ethical judgements remain suspended in a vacuum. As H. Richard Niebuhr has pointed out, all our values are held in relation to a centre of value," (Wogaman JP, 1976: 2).

And the centre of value discussed by Wogaman is Jesus Christ. The book of Isaiah 11:1, explains the coming of Christ Jesus shall be as a stump. "A shoot shall come out from the stump of Jesse, and a branch shall grow out of his roots."

I have discussed the South African public's involvement in the demise of the country. We have voted corruption into government, on two occasions in the Jacob Zuma era, simply because we believed the lie that pensioners will lose the R1500.00 grant money.

Secondly we have deviated from God's command. Our history is like that of the Israelites in the Bible; they were rescued by God from Egypt, to the Promised land, out into captivity in Babylon, rescued into Judea and Israel, back into captivity in Concentration Camps in Europe and ultimately back in their land.

The reason for this is that, out of the entire nation of the Israelites, some decided to repent and associated themselves with God. That same

God has thrown us a life line in Jesus Christ. All we need to do is to confess our sins, be cleansed in the blood of Christ. Psalm 37:4 says "Delight in the Lord and he will give you the desires of your heart." I believe every one of us harbours a desire for a life free of poverty. God is the answer.

The Ingonyama Trust

Just as I was about to rap up this book and send to the printers, The Mail and Guardian, 8 to 15 August 2019, published a story that actually explains how Ingonyama Trust was started.

Under the heading, "The IFP, the king and the secret 1994 election deal" and the subheading, "Ingonyama Trust: the full story revealed at last." Pages 4 & 5.

In there it is revealed that a few days before the 1994 first democratic non-racial elections, the then chief Mangosuthu Buthelezi leader of Inkatha cultural organisation, threatened to go on extended rampage and kill more blacks if a piece of land now known as Ingonyama Trust is not reserved for the Zulu nation under the king. It is reported in the newspaper that this deal was signed by FW de Klerk and Zulu king Goodwill Zwelithini in the absence of the ANC led by Nelson Mandela.

While we talk of the Biblical Stump in Jesus Christ, we now talk of the Apartheid stump, Kwazulu-Natal Province, that was meticulously calculated to twist the arms of both the ANC under Nelson Mandela and Apartheid regime under FW de Klerk. I say twist their arms because it would have ignited time bomb to have changed the election date from 27 April 1994. Or for that matter, refuse to accede to this malicious demand. There were ten homelands in South Africa, nine were incorporated in the new South Africa, except one, by holding Black South African life to ransom. I pray God to preserve Chief Mangosuthu Buthelezi and king Goodwill Zwelithini to live endlessly until they rectify this malady.

We pray that the expropriation of land without compensation will be resolved peacefully.

We live everyday with the faith in our Triune God, God the Father, God the Son and God the Holy Spirit, that He will reunite blacks and live in everlasting peace. He has His way of guiding the guilty to a moving expose of confession, just like He did with the iniquitous king David in Israel. He first vehemently denied, but went on to compose Psalm 51. It feels like David was crying like a baby when he scribbled this psalm.

There's a saying that goes, God hasn't got an enemy, His enemy is God-self. This is derived from the Sesotho hymn that says, "Empa bohale ba hao le ha bo ka tota, bo tingwa ke mohau ha re sokoloha…Even though Your wrath may overwhelm You, it is quelled by Your Grace, provided we repent." This means in the unthinkable instance of His fountain of never ending love running dry, His never ending fountain of Grace takes over, until that of love is filled again and the process repeats itself; for our sake.

We look forward to that day in South Africa. That's my unwavering faith.

Reference List:

Bosch DJ. 1993. Reflections on Biblical Models of mission. In Phillips & Coote 1993: 175-192

GND: The Good News Bible

JCM: The John C. Maxwell Bible

TEEC, 2011: Ethics, Booklet 1. Turffontein, Gauteng

Wogaman JP. 1976, A Christian Method of Moral Judgement. Western Printing Services Ltd Bristol

SPEECH BY PRESIDENT NELSON MAN-DELA AT THE INAUGURATION OF THE CONSTITUTIONAL COURT

Johannesburg, 14 February 1995
President of the Constitutional Court;
Chief Justice;
Honourable Judges;
Distinguished guests;
Ladies and gentleman.

1. The last time I appeared in court was to hear whether or not I was going to
2. be sentenced to death. Fortunately for myself and my colleagues we were
3. not. Today I rise not as an accused but, on behalf of behalf of the people of
4. South Africa, to inaugurate a court South Africa has never had, a court on
5. which hinges the future of our democracy.
6. It is not just a building that we inaugurate, handsome though it is. It is not a
7. body of wise men and women that we launch on their path, important
8. though we regard their work. It is not just our blessings that we give to their
9. work, confident as we are in their integrity and commitment to justice. It is
10. an institution that we establish - South Africa's first Constitutional Court.
11. People come and people go. Customs, fashions, and preferences change.
12. Yet the web of fundamental rights and justice which a nation proclaims,

13. must not be broken. It is the task of this court to ensure that the values of
14. freedom and equality which underlie our interim constitution - and which
15. will surely be embodied in our final constitution - are nurtured and
16. protected so that they may endure.
17. We expect you to stand on guard not only against direct assault on the
18. principles of the constitution, but against insidious corrosion. Attacks on the
19. basic rights of the people are invariably couched in innocent language.
20. We do pledge that the new Government of National Unity will never be
21. party to the subterfuges of the past which put a humane gloss over the
22. most iniquitous denials of our rights. We are confident that the new
23. parliament, imbued with openness of debate and honesty of purpose, will
24. never attempt to pass laws which oppress and divide. We believe in the
25. constitution and the processes it has established. We are convinced that
26. multi-party democracy and freedom of opinion have taken firm root in our
27. country. We have no doubt that the nation is committed irreversibly to
28. acknowledging diversity and respecting the basic rights of everyone.
29. Yet experience everywhere teaches that in addition to all this, special
30. institutions are required to ensure the continuity of right and justice.
31. We have fought hard for the basic principles enshrined in the interim
32. constitution. The rights and freedoms it proclaims are not simply words
33. taken from hallowed texts in other parts of the world. They represent our
34. endeavours, and our dreams of a free and just society.
35. The interim constitution, and the principles it sets out for the Constitutional
36. Assembly, are homegrown. They took root in the soil of our own harsh
37. experiences. They grew upwards towards the light of our own highest
38. aspirations. We must defend them, all of us.
39. Our constitution rests on three fundamental pillars: Parliament, the
40. Government, and the Constitutional Court. Each has its specific role to play.
41. Take away or undermine any, and you weaken the whole structure. That is
42. why your independence is guaranteed in the constitution.
43. One of the things one discovers when coming into office is that there is no
44. shortage of rubber stamps. South Africans did not establish this court to be
45. another rubber stamp. We expect you to be creative and independent. We
46. expect you to be true to the oath you have just sworn.
47. Constitutionalism means that no office and no institution can be higher

48. than the law. The highest and the most humble in the land all, without
49. exception, owe allegiance to the same document, the same principles. It
50. does not matter whether you are black or white, male or female, young or
51. old;whether you speak Tswana or Afrikaans;whether you are rich or poor or
52. ride in a smart new car or walk barefoot;whether you wear a uniform or are
53. locked up in a cell. We all have certain basic rights, and those fundamental
54. rights are set out in the Constitution.
55. The authority of government comes from the people through the
56. Constitution. Your tasks and responsibilities, as well as your power, come to
57. you from the people through the Constitution. The people speak through
58. the Constitution. The Constitution enables the multiple voices of the people
59. to be heard in an organized, articulate, meaningful and principled manner.
60. We trust that you will find the means through your judgments to speak
61. directly to the people.
62. You are a new court in every way. The process whereby you were selected
63. was new. When we look at you, we see for the first time the many
64. dimensions of our rich and varied country. We see a multiplicity of
65. backgrounds and life experiences. Your tasks are new. Your powers are
66. new. We hope that, without abandoning the many sterling virtues of legal
67. tradition, you will find a new way of expressing the great truths of your
68. calling. You will be dealing with the rights of millions of ordinary people.
69. The Constitution which you will be serving is the product of their sacrifice
70. and belief. I am sure that I am speaking for all of them when I say that the
71. basic reasons for your decisions should be spelt out in a language that all
72. can understand.
73. The success of the Constitutional Court will depend in large measure on the
74. successful functioning of the ordinary courts. Every court, from the most
75. isolated magistrate's court to the Appeal Court in Bloemfontein, has a role
76. to play. The letter and the spirit of the Constitution must permeate every
77. aspect of justice in our country.
78. A particularly heavy responsibility rests on the Appellate Division, to ensure
79. that legislation is interpreted, and that the common law and custom are
80. developed, in the light of the principles enunciated in the Constitution. We
81. envisage an active and fruitful partnership between the ordinary courts and
82. the Constitutional Court.

83. To Judge Arthur Chaskalson and other members of the Constitutional Court
84. let me say the following: yours is the most noble task that could fall to any
85. legal person. In the last resort, the guarantee of the fundamental rights and
86. freedoms for which we have fought so hard, lies in your hands. We look to
87. you to honour the Constitution and the people it represents. We expect
88. from you, no, demand of you, the greatest use of your wisdom, honesty and
89. good sense - no short cuts, no easy solutions. Your work is not only lofty, it
90. is also lonely.
91. In the end you have only the Constitution and your conscience on which
92. you can rely. We look upon you to serve both without fear or favour.